# Praise for this book

'A quietly formidable achievement; its understated
evocation of tragedy and strength in the face of
victimization make it a graceful classic.'

*Women's Review*

'Powerfully political.'

*Poetry Nation Review*

'Nawal El Saadawi's achievement is to lay bare the
thin flesh and huge passions of her characters.'

*West Indian Digest*

# About this Series

NAWAL EL SAADAWI's writing has the power to shock, move, inform and inspire. Her powerful stories of the lives of ordinary women in the Middle East remain as relevant today as when they were first published a quarter of a century ago.

In *Woman at Point Zero*, one of her earliest novels, she tells the tragic story of Firdaus's descent into prostitution and her defiance in the face of disapproval and condemnation. *God Dies by the Nile* is a powerful allegory about Zakeya, a peasant farmer, and her shocking act of revenge on corrupt village elders. *The Hidden Face of Eve* – part autobiography and part polemic – is a brutal exposé of the treatment of women in the Arab world. The first book by an Arab woman to talk openly about female genital mutilation, it encompasses sex, love, marriage, fertility and divorce, as well as Arab women in history and literature, in its panorama.

Saadawi herself was born in 1931 in a small village outside Cairo. Unusually, she was sent to school and later trained as a doctor. Her writing was inspired by her experiences of treating women in her medical practice. A vociferous political activist, Saadawi has been imprisoned in and exiled from Egypt, and put herself forward as a candidate for presidential election there in 2004. Her work has been internationally acclaimed, and she has been awarded numerous honorary doctorates and prizes.

These beautifully designed reissues are classics of contemporary Middle Eastern literature which will engage a new generation of readers.

# About the Author

NAWAL EL SAADAWI was born in 1931, in a small village outside Cairo. Unusually, she and her brothers and sisters were educated together, and she graduated from the University of Cairo Medical School in 1955, specializing in psychiatry. For two years, she practised as a medical doctor, both at the university and in her native Tahla. Her first book, *Memoirs of a Woman Doctor*, was published in Cairo in 1958.

From 1963 until 1972, Saadawi worked for the Egyptian government as Director General for Public Health Education. During this time, she also studied at Columbia University in New York, where she received her Master's degree in Public Health in 1966. In 1972, however, she lost her job in the Egyptian government as a result of political pressure. The magazine *Health*, which she founded and had edited for more than three years, was closed down.

From 1973 to 1978 Saadawi worked at the High Institute of Literature and Science. It was at this time that she began to write, in works of fiction and non-fiction, the books on the oppression of Arab women for which she has become famous. Her most renowned novel, *Woman at Point Zero*, was published in Beirut in 1973. It was followed in 1976 by *God Dies by the Nile* and in 1977 by her study of Arab women, *The Hidden Face of Eve*.

In 1981 Nawal El Saadawi publicly criticized the one-party rule of President Anwar Sadat, and was subsequently arrested and imprisoned. She was released one month after Sadat's assassination. In 1982, she established the Arab Women's Solidarity Association, which was outlawed in 1991. When, in 1988, her name appeared on a fundamentalist death list, she and her second husband, Sherif Hetata, fled to the USA, where she taught at Duke University and Washington State University.

Saadawi returned to Egypt in 1996. In 2004 she presented herself as a candidate for the presidential elections in Egypt, with a platform of human rights, democracy and greater freedom for women. In July 2005, however, she was forced to withdraw her candidacy in the face of ongoing government persecution.

Nawal El Saadawi has achieved widespread international recognition for her work. She holds honorary doctorates from the universities of York, Illinois at Chicago, St Andrews and Tromso. Her many prizes and awards include the Great Minds of the Twentieth Century Prize, awarded by the American Biographical Institute in 2003, the North–South Prize from the Council of Europe and the Premi Internacional Catalunya in 2004. Her books have been translated into over twenty-eight languages worldwide. They are taught in universities across the world.

She now works as a writer, psychiatrist and activist. Her most recent novel, entitled *Al Riwaya* (The Novel) was published in Cairo in 2004.

# God Dies by the Nile

NAWAL EL SAADAWI

*Translated by Sherif Hetata*

ZED BOOKS
*London & New York*

*God Dies by the Nile* was first published in Arabic in Beirut
in 1974, under the title *The Death of the Only Man on Earth*,
and first published in English in 1985 by Zed Books Ltd,
7 Cynthia Street, London N1 9JF, UK,
and Room 400, 175 Fifth Avenue, New York, NY 10010, USA
www.zedbooks.co.uk

This new edition was first published in 2007

Designed and typeset in ITC Bodoni Twelve
by illuminati, Grosmont, www.illuminatibooks.co.uk
Cover designed by Andrew Corbett
Printed and bound in Malta by Gutenberg Press Ltd

Distributed in the USA exclusively by Palgrave Macmillan, a division
of St Martin's Press, LLC, 175 Fifth Avenue, New York, NY 10010

A catalogue record for this book is available from the British Library
Library of Congress Cataloging-in-Publication Data available

ISBN   978 1 84277 876 0 Hb
ISBN   978 1 84277 877 7 Pb

# Foreword

I was six or seven years of age when I heard about a poor peasant girl who drowned herself in the Nile – she had been working in the house of the village mayor. My grandmother whispered something that I didn't understand in my mother's ear. At the age of ten I heard about another girl who fled during the night. She was a servant in the same house, fourteen years old and pregnant. Nobody accused the mayor, except a young peasant who had been planning to marry the girl. He was shot in the fields and no-one was captured. In a dream, I saw the mayor in prison accused of raping servant girls and robbing the women of their harvest. When I told my grandmother, she said it was impossible, that the mayor was a god and no-one could punish him. She said that the mayor exploited the peasants to serve the king's interest, and the king exploited the mayor and the peasants to serve the interests of the British army in the Suez canal. The word 'god' echoed around me but I didn't know its real meaning and I instinctively didn't like it. My parents gave my brother more freedom and more food than me, though I was better at school and helped my mother more. When I asked why, they told me that it is what God said. I felt that God was unjust like the mayor and the king, and that he deserved to be punished, but I kept this to myself.

These women and men in my village inspired me to write *God Dies by the Nile.* Zakeya is not very different from my grandmother and my aunts, relatives and neighbours. In addition to the oppression of colonial rule at that time, women were oppressed by men in the family, in society and in the streets. Poor women were more vulnerable than rich women.

In 1972 I published my first non-fiction book about women and sex. It was banned by the authorities and I was promptly dismissed from my post in the government. I found myself at home with nothing to do but write. I wrote fiction partly because I enjoyed it more, and partly because it seemed less likely to be banned – most of the censors were half-literate civil servants on low salaries, I did not imagine that they would read novels. I sat alone in my small apartment in Giza thinking about my new novel. I don't know why my childhood memory came back to me, especially the image of the mayor and his men sitting smoking by the banks of the Nile, looking at the girls walking past with jars on their heads. The faces of my grandmother and other poor women in my family appeared vividly to me. I finished the novel in two months. Writing it gave me enormous pleasure, a pleasure which sustained me inside prison, and which is more essential to me than breathing.

At that time, Sadat was pursuing his so-called 'open door policy', opening Egypt to foreign, especially American, goods and investment. The result was increased poverty, unemployment, religious fundamentalism and the veiling of and discrimination against women. The Islamization of Egypt went hand in hand with the Americanization. The shops sold imported veils from the USA and Saudi Arabia and prayer mats from Mecca, alongside red lipstick and tight blue jeans. The majority of people in Egypt were deprived of their basic material needs. Our television screens were flooded with religious men preaching chastity, modesty, spirituality and the veil, interspersed with adverts that used naked women's bodies to sell imported foreign goods. For women, the veil and female genital mutilation came to be part of authentic Islamic identity. I found it impossible to be silent. I published my articles in opposition newspapers and eventually found myself in prison, accused of betraying Egypt. One month later, however, in 1981, Sadat was assassinated and I was released by the new president.

*God Dies by the Nile* didn't escape this climate of censorship and oppression. Like most of my work, it had to be published in Lebanon. My Lebanese publisher in Beirut changed the title to *Death of the Only Man on Earth*. He told me that God cannot die, and when I tried to explain that the word god is a symbol for the head of the village, he said 'Yes, I know, but religious fanatics will not understand this and will burn my publishing house.' This actually happened several years later. In 1982 *God Dies by the Nile* was published, with another fourteen of my books, by a publisher called Madbouli in Cairo. He used the Lebanese title. He said 'They will burn my publishing house if I publish a book with a title like that. God does not die, he lives eternally.'

Thus the book was never published in Arabic with its original title, although it is reprinted to this day. Ten editions at least have come out since I wrote it. I think many women and men still read it. I have received many letters from readers saying that the village in the novel did not differ much from their village.

Some men were angry and accused me of mocking Islam and encouraging heresy.

Though it was written more than thirty years ago, I feel that *God Dies by the Nile* still describes the life of peasant women and men in Egypt. The existing regime is no better than the Sadat regime – even worse. Poverty, American neocolonialism and religious fundamentalism have continued to rise. I visit my village every now and then and I see that it still resembles Zakeya's village. Perhaps this is why people still read the book and why publishers still reprint it. The novel has been translated into many languages, including English, and I'm glad that its original title has not been changed. God still dies by the Nile.

*Nawal El Saadawi*
*Cairo, 2006*

# Glossary

*Ame*   Baby talk for 'Shame on you!'

*daya*   Local midwife.

*Eid*   Festival following the Ramadan fast.

*galabeya*   Long, wide garment reaching to the ankles, worn by peasant women and men alike, with differences in the cut, material and colours.

*Hejaz*   Mecca.

*jiba*   Garment worn over a caftan, made of thicker, darker material.

*melaya*   A long wrap of black silk worn around the body.

*Misr*   The central government in Cairo which manages national affairs. Misr, here, is Egypt, but also refers to the capital.

*mouloukheya*   A vegetable used to make a thick, green, garlicky soup. The long, resilient stalk is used in the villages to induce abortions by pushing it into the neck of the uterus.

*Sunna*   Islamic jurisprudence, used to develop and explain Islamic teachings embodied in the Koran and the sayings of the Prophet Mohamed. The four prostrations mentioned here are not considered canonical but only optional. Practised as an additional rite, they testify to greater religious fervour and should bring more blessings.

*tabla*  A long, conical drum.

*tambour*  A primitive water-wheel turned by hand.

*yoo yoos*  A prolonged trilling sound meant to express joy.

*zar*  A form of exorcism to rid a person (usually a woman) of an evil spirit by means of a frenzied dance accompanied by incantations and verses of the Koran.

# I

Before the crimson rays of dawn touched the treetops, before the cry of the cock, the bark of a dog, or the bray of a donkey pierced through the heavy darkness, or the voice of 'Sheikh Hamzawi' echoed in the silence with the first call to prayer, the big wooden door opened slowly, creaking, with the rusty sound of an ancient water-wheel. A tall, upright shadow slipped through and advanced on two legs with a powerful steady stride. Behind, followed a second shadow, on four legs which seemed to bend beneath it, as it slouched forwards with a lazy, ambling gait.

The two shadows disappeared into the darkness to emerge out of it again over the river bank. Zakeya's face stood out in the pale light of dawn, gaunt, severe, bloodless. The lips were tightly closed, resolute, as though no word could ever pass through them. The large, wide-open eyes fixed on the horizon expressed an angry defiance. Behind her, the head of the buffalo nodded up and down, its face gaunt and bloodless, but not unkind, its wide-open eyes humble, broken, resigned to whatever lay ahead.

The light of dawn glimmered on the river, revealing the minute waves, like tiny wrinkles in an old, sad, silent face. Deep underneath, its waters seemed immobile, their flow as imperceptible as a moment of passing time, or the slow movement of the clouds in the dark sky.

In the wide-open spaces the air, too, was hushed and silent. It slipped through the branches of the trees so gently that they barely moved, but it continued to carry the fine, invisible particles of dust from over the high bank of the river, down the slope to the dark, mud huts huddled in rows, their tiny windows closed, their low, uneven roofs stacked with mounds of dry cotton sticks, cakes of dung and straw, then further down into the narrow twisting lanes and alleys blocked with manure, and on to the stream which completed the village contour, where they settled to form a dark, slimy, oozing layer covering its green water.

Zakeya continued to walk with the buffalo behind her, her legs moving at the same unchanging pace, as unchanging as the set look on her face, as the immobile waters of the river to her left, as everything else in these last moments of the night. But to her right there was a slow shift as the mud huts started to pass behind, and the fields emerged before her eyes like a green ribbon laid out parallel to the Nile.

She advanced between the two stretches of green and brown with the same swinging movement starting from the hips and thighs. Overhead, the black night withdrew gradually as the crimson hue of dawn spread out, then, after a while, changed to a glaring, orange light. Suddenly, over the edge of the earth a point of sun shone out, grew slowly to become a disc of fire, then climbed up into the sky. But before the light of day had chased away the night, Zakeya had already reached her field, tied the buffalo to the water-wheel beside the stream, removed her black shawl and put it on the ground, rolled up her sleeves, and tied the tail of her *galabeya* around her waist.

Now her hoe could be heard, thudding out over the neighbouring fields with a steady sound, as it cut deep into the ground. The muscles in her arms stood out, and below the black *galabeya* knotted tightly around her waist, the long powerful legs showed naked and brown in the morning light; the features of her face were still the same, still sharp, still gaunt, no longer pale, but dark with the leathery tan bitten into them by heat and dust, and sun and open space. Yet deep underneath was the same pallor which her skin revealed before and now concealed. Her body no longer stood upright. It was bent over the hoe as she dug away in the soil. Her eyes did not look at the ground, were not fixed to her feet. They were the same. They had not changed. They were raised, fixed to some distant point with the same angry defiance which looked out of them before. And the blows of her hoe seemed to echo with an anger buried deep down as she lifted it high up in the air and swung it down with all her might into the soil.

Its blows resounded with their regular sound like the muffled strokes of a clock striking out the hour. They devoured time, moved forwards machine-like, cut into the earth hour after hour. They never tired, never broke down, or gasped for breath, or sought respite. They went on with a steady thud, thud, thud echoing in the neighbouring fields throughout the day, almost inhuman, relentless, frightening in the fury of their power. Even at midday, when the men broke off for a meal and an hour of rest, they went on without a stop. The buffalo might cease turning round and round for a short while, and the water-wheel would stop creaking for a moment, but her hoe kept on falling and rising, rising and falling from sky to earth, and earth to sky.

The sun rose up in the sky gradually. Its disc turned into a ball of fire, choking the wind, bearing down on the trees, turning everything into solid dryness, so that all things seemed to suffocate, burn in its red fire, and dry up, except the rivulets of sweat pouring down from Zakeya's face and body on to the ground. Beneath the sweat her face was livid like the face of the buffalo turning round and round beneath its yoke.

The hours passed. The sun began to lean towards the earth in a slow, sweeping movement. Its flames no longer burned with the same ire. The heat subsided, and the air stirred, wafting a soft breeze with it from the waters of the Nile. The tree tops swayed from side to side unwillingly, as though spent out. Once more the sky was bathed in a glaring, orange light, gradually swept aside by the sad, grey hue of beginning twilight. The sweat on her face dried up leaving a layer of dust behind like ashes on a dying fire. She threw the hoe on one side, stretched the muscles of her back and stood upright. She looked around for a moment as though awakened in the night, then rolled down her sleeves and untied the knotted folds of her long, black garment before letting it drop down over her legs to the ground. She drew the shawl around her head, and stepped out of the field on to the dusty track. A few moments later she was once more a dark shadow walking back over the same path, with the same steady step, and with the buffalo plodding slowly behind. Now the green expanses of the fields were to her left, and the brown waters of the Nile on her right. In the distance the trees had become slender black silhouettes etched against the greying sky. The sun had dropped below the earth, and to the west, its crimson light no longer fought against the dusk.

# God Dies by the Nile

The two shadows travelled slowly over the dusty track on the river bank. Her shadow was the same: tall, upright with the head rising straight above the neck. It moved as though advancing to attack. The second shadow too had not changed one bit. It slouched along, completely spent, its step resigned, its head still bent. They advanced over the river bank, two silent shadows in the deepening night. Nothing moved in the whole wide world around, nothing moaned or sighed or cried or even spoke. Only silence in the silent night spreading its cloak over the fields stretched out on the other side, over the waters of the Nile, over the sky above their heads, over everything on the ground.

Slowly the fields swung back behind them, and the huts emerged in front, small, dark, indistinct shadows huddling up for support or shelter against the river bank or perhaps afraid of sliding down into the dust-covered expanse of low land.

The two shadows descended the slope into the ditch, and got lost in the narrow twisting lanes, as they glided furtively along between the houses. They came to a stop in front of the big wooden door. Zakeya opened it with a push of her powerful fist and it gave way with a heavy creaking sound. She dropped the rope by which she held the buffalo. It ambled in through the open door and went on towards the stable. She watched it go in for a moment, then squatted in the entrance to the house with her back up against the wall and her eyes facing the open door, so that she could see the part of the lane which lay beyond it.

She sat immobile, her eyes staring into the darkness as though fixed on something she perceived in front of her. Perhaps what had caught her attention was nothing but a mound of manure piled up near the entrance to her house, or the stools of a child, lying on the ground, where it had squatted to relieve itself near

5

the wall, or an army of ants swarming around the body of a dead beetle, or one of the black iron columns in the huge door on the opposite side of the lane.

The darkness was all pervading, almost impenetrable, but she continued to stare into the night until a moment came when she felt a stabbing pain in her head. She pulled the shawl even more tightly around it, but after a while the pain travelled down to her stomach. She put out her hand and fumbled in the dark for the flat, straw basket containing the week's store of food. She pulled it up to her side, parted her tightly closed lips and began to feed little pieces of dry bread, dry cheese and salted pickles into her mouth.

Her lids were heavy with an exhaustion which was over-whelming. She dozed off for short moments, her head resting on her knees. She could no longer see anything in the total darkness, even when her eyes were wide open. Kafrawi slipped in through the big wooden door and squatted down beside her. She was looking straight at him as he came up, so he thought she had seen him. But although wide awake she had not really seen the man he has become. His body shrinks before her eyes to that of a small boy, and now she is looking at him through her child's eyes, as she crawls on her belly over the dust-covered yard of their house, panting breathlessly, with her tongue hanging out of her mouth. The dust gets into her eyes, and nose and mouth. She sits up and starts rubbing her little fists into her eyes. The next moment she stops rubbing her eyes, and sits with her hands in her lap looking around, but suddenly she sees four black hoofs moving over the ground towards her. One of the hoofs rises slowly up into the air. She can see its dark forbidding underside like the surface of a big hammer ready to drop with all its might on her head. A shiver goes through her, and she screams out loud. Two strong arms reach out to her and lift her from the ground. The feel of her mother's arms around her, the warmth of her breast, and the smell of her flesh are reassuring and her screams subside.

She could no longer remember her mother's face; the features had faded away in her mind. Only the smell of her body remained alive. Something about it reminded her of the smell of dough, or of yeast. And whenever this smell was in the air around her, a strong feeling of happiness came over her. Her face would soften and grow tender for a short moment, but an instant later it would become as harsh, and as resolute, as it had been throughout her life.

When she learnt to stand on her legs, and walk, they allowed her to go to the fields with Kafrawi. He walked in front leading the buffalo by a rope tied round its neck, while she brought up the rear driving the donkey with its load of manure. Her brother remained silent all the way. She never heard his voice except when he urged the buffalo on with the cry 'Shee, shee' or tried to make the donkey move faster by shouting 'Haa, haa' at it.

She remembered seeing her father standing in the fields, but could not recall his face. All that remained of him in her memory was a pair of long, thin, spindly legs, with protruding knees, a *galabeya* with its tail lifted and tied around his waist, a huge hoe held tightly in his big hands, as it rose and fell with a regular thud, and the sombre, heavy creaking of the water-wheel. The wheeze of the water-wheel would continue to go round and round inside her. At certain moments she could feel it stop suddenly, make her turn towards the buffalo and cry out 'Shee, shee', but the animal would not budge. It stood there motionless. The black head perfectly still, the black eyes staring at her fixedly.

Zakeya was about to repeat 'Shee, shee' when she realized the face was not that of the buffalo, but Kafrawi's. He resembled her a great deal. His features were carved like hers, his eyes large, black and also full of anger, but it was a different kind of anger, mingling in their depths with despair, and expressing a profound humiliation.

He remained seated by her side, his lips tightly closed, his back pressed up against the mud wall, his eyes staring into the darkness of the lane, reaching across to the bars in the huge iron door facing them some distance away. He turned towards her and parting his lips slightly spoke in a harsh whisper.

'The girl has disappeared, Zakeya. She is gone.'

'Gone!?' she asked in anguish.

'Yes, gone. There is no trace of her in the whole village.'

He sounded desperate. She stared at him out of her large, black eyes. He held her stare, but there was a profound hopelessness in the way he looked back at her.

'Nefissa is nowhere to be found in Kafr El Teen, Zakeya,' he said. 'She's vanished completely. She will never return.'

He held his head in his hands and added, this time almost in a wail, 'She's lost, Zakeya. Oh, my God.'

Zakeya looked away from him, and fixed her eyes on the lane, then whispered in a mechanical way, her voice full of sadness, 'We've lost her the same as we lost Galal.'

He lifted his face and murmured, 'Galal is not lost, Zakeya. He will return to you soon.'

'Every day you say the same thing, Kafrawi. You know that Galal is dead and you're trying to convince me that he's not.'

'No one has told us that he is dead.'

'Many of them died, Kafrawi, so why not him?'

'But many have come back. Be patient and pray Allah, that he may send him back safely to us.'

'I've prayed so many times, so many times,' she said in a choking voice.

'Pray again, Zakeya. Pray to Allah that he may return safely, and Nefissa too. Where could the girl have gone? Where?'

Their voices like the successive gasps of two people in pain ceased abruptly. Silence descended upon them, a silence heavier than the thick cloak of darkness around them. Their eyes continued to stare fixedly into the limitless night, and neither of them moved. They sat on, side by side, as immobile as the mud huts buried in the dark.

# II

The big iron door swung open slowly, and the Mayor of Kafr El Teen stepped out into the lane. He was tall with big, hefty shoulders and a broad, almost square face. Its upper half had come to him from his mother: smooth silky hair, and deep blue eyes which stared out from under a prominent, high forehead. The lower half came from the upper reaches of the country in the south, and had been handed down to him by his father: thick, jet black whiskers overhung by a coarse nose, below which the lips were soft and fleshy, suggesting lust rather than sensuality. His eyes had a haughty, almost arrogant quality, like those of an English gentleman accustomed to command. When he spoke his voice was hoarse, and unrefined, like that of an Upper Egyptian peasant. But its hoarseness was endowed with a mellow, humble quality that belied any hint of the aggression often found in the voices of men cowed by years of oppression in former colonies like Egypt and India.

He moved with a slow step, his long, dark cloak falling to the ground. Behind him followed the Chief of the Village Guard

and the Sheikh of the mosque. As they came out they could see
two shadows squatting in the dark across the lane. The faces
were invisible but the three men knew that it was Kafrawi and
his sister, Zakeya, for they were in the habit of sitting there,
side by side, for long hours without exchanging a single word.
When there was only one shadow instead of two, it meant that
Kafrawi had stayed behind in the fields, where he would labour
until sunrise.

At this hour they were in the habit of going to the nearby
mosque for evening prayers. Once back, they would install themselves on the terrace of the mayor's house overlooking the river,
or saunter down to the shop owned by Haj Ismail, the village
barber. There they sat smoking and chatting as each one in turn
drew in a puff from the long, cane stem of the water-jar pipe.

But this time the Mayor refused to smoke the water-jar pipe.
Instead he extracted a cigar from his side pocket, bit off the
end, lit it with a match, and started to smoke while the others
watched. Haj Ismail could tell from the way the Mayor frowned
that he was not in a good mood. So he disappeared into his shop
and a moment later came back, sidled up close to him, and tried
to slip a small piece of hashish into the palm of his hand, but the
Mayor pushed it away and said, 'No, no. Not tonight.'

'But why, your highness?' enquired Haj Ismail.

'Did you not hear the news?'

'What news, your highness?'

'The news about the government.'

'Which government, your highness?'

'Haj Ismail! How many governments do you think we have?'

'A good number.'

'Nonsense! We have only one government, and you know
that very well.'

'Which government do you have in mind, the government of Misr or the government of Kafr El Teen?'

'The government of Misr, of course.'

'Where do we come in then?'

The Chief of the Village Guard laughed out loud and exclaimed, 'Who would dare deny that we're just as much of a government ourselves?'

It was Sheikh Hamzawi's turn to laugh. His tobacco-stained teeth could be seen protruding from his big mouth, and the yellow-beaded rosary swayed from side to side as he slipped it furiously through his fingers.

But the Mayor did not join in the laughter. He closed his thick lips tightly around his cigar, and his blue eyes gazed into the distance over the long ribbon of the river water and the wide expanses of cultivated land, now invisible in the darkness. In his mind he could see them stretching out between the two villages of Kafr El Teen and El Rawla. When he used to visit the area with his mother during the summer months, he never imagined that some day he would settle down in Kafr El Teen. He loved the city life of Cairo. The lamps shining on the dark surface of the tarmac roads. The coloured lights of the riverside casinos reflected in the flowing waters of the Nile. The nightclubs thronged with people eating and drinking as they sat around the tables, the women dancing, their bodies moving, their perfume and soft laughter going through him.

At the time he was still a college student. But unlike his elder brother he hated lectures, and lecture rooms, hated the talk about knowledge, and his future. Above all, he hated listening to his brother discoursing about politics and political groupings.

As they sat there plunged in silence, Haj Ismail suddenly remembered the morning newspaper he had left in the shop on the wooden table next to the weighing machine. He disappeared inside again and returned carrying it folded up in his hand. He opened it out under the kerosene lamp, and started to read the headlines on the front page, but his attention was drawn away from them by the picture of a man. It stood out clearly in the middle of the page. The features were familiar and it did not take him long to realize that he was looking at the elder brother of the Mayor. He tried to read what was written below, but the print was too small, and he could not make out what it said. He hesitated for a moment, then moving closer to the Mayor whispered in his ear in as low a voice as possible.

'Has the news you mentioned got something to do with your brother?'

After a brief silence the Mayor said, 'Yes.'

This time Haj Ismail's question expressed concern. 'Has some misfortune befallen him?'

There was a note of pride in the Mayor's voice as he replied, 'No, on the contrary.'

Haj Ismail was so excited he could barely contain himself. 'Does your highness mean to say that he's been elevated to a higher post?'

The Mayor blew out a dense cloud of smoke. 'Yes, exactly, Haj Ismail.'

Haj Ismail clapped his hands together with glee, then looked around at the others and said, 'Our friends, then we must drink sherbet to celebrate the occasion.'

A flutter went round the men seated in front of the shop. The newspaper quickly changed hands going from one to the other. Haj Ismail left them and came back carrying a bottle of sherbet and empty cups.

But the Mayor seemed to be lost in his thoughts. All day he

had kept wondering why the moment he had seen his brother's picture in the newspaper a feeling of inadequacy and depression had come over him. He knew this feeling well. It was always accompanied by a bitterness of the mouth, a dryness of the throat which turned into a burning sensation as it moved down to his chest, followed by an obscure and yet sharp pain which radiated outwards from his stomach.

He was a small boy when this feeling first started to come over him. He remembered how he used to run to the bathroom and vomit all the food in his stomach. Then he would stand there examining himself in the mirror above the washbasin. His face was deathly pale, his lips almost yellow, and the gleam which shone in his eyes was gone. They looked dull, apathetic, resigned, as though some cloud had descended upon them and snuffed out their liveliness.

He would wash his mouth several times to dispel the remaining taste of bitterness which lingered behind. When he raised his head to look into the mirror, it was his brother's face that appeared before him. He contemplated the rosy cheeks, the gleam of victory in the eyes. In his ears rang the exultant tones of the voice he knew so well. 'I succeed in everything I undertake. But you have been a failure all the time.'

He would spit out the water in his mouth on to the face smiling calmly at him from the mirror. Then lift his neck, square his shoulders, and addressing it in a loud voice say, 'I am a thousand times better than you.'

Anyone seeing him as he walked out of the bathroom door would imagine that of the two he was no doubt the more successful. His lips had regained their rosy colour, and his eyes were shining brightly. The bitter taste in his mouth had gone, and once more his merry laughter rang out, as he romped around mischievously, teasing his mother who sat in her armchair knitting, trying to pull at the tip of the thread and make the woollen skein roll out. Her haughty blue eyes would flash with an angry light and the curt sentence pronounced with an English accent would sting his pride. 'Your brother is much better than you are.'

Sometimes she would set aside her needles, reach out for the folded newspaper lying on the table next to her, and pointing to a name printed in small letters on one of the pages inside, would say, 'Your brother has passed his examinations brilliantly, whereas you...'

He would stop laughing immediately, as though something had seized him by the throat and was choking him, then swallow several times without responding. And just as suddenly he would realize that he was not really happy, that he had been forcing himself into a merry mood. This feeling of being superior to his brother was just a disguise. The truth was so overwhelming that it shook him to the marrow of his bones. It seemed to exude from every pore in his body with the cold, sticky sweat that now ran under his clothes. It crept into his mouth and nose, reviving the taste of bitterness once more, dropped down with it to his chest, then through a small hole into his belly. He would run back to the bathroom and vomit repeatedly until there was nothing left for him to vomit.

Haj Ismail was sipping his second round of sherbet from the copper cup when he noticed the Mayor spit on the ground scornfully, then he straightened his back, lifted his head, and his eyes travelled slowly over them with a haughty stare. His look seemed to say, 'Compared to me, you people are just nobodies. I am from a noble family. My mother is English, and my brother is one of the people who rule this country.'

Haj Ismail cringed as he sat on the bench, as though trying to make himself so small that he could avoid the eyes of the Mayor. He had been on the verge of joking with him, of telling him the latest stories, but immediately thought better of it. His eyes kept shifting backwards and forwards between the picture of the Mayor's elder brother sitting in the midst of the most important people in the country, his features expressing a haughty arrogance and the small shop with its old, cracked shelves, covered in dust, and the few rusty tins standing dejectedly on them. He tried to tear himself away from the comparison only to find himself lost in the contemplation of the Mayor's expensive cloak, while his hand kept fingering the coarse fabric of his own *galabeya*.

The Mayor's eyes caught Haj Ismail in the act of lifting his cup of sherbet to his lips and draining it in one quick gulp, as though it was a purge of castor oil. He burst out laughing, slapped him jocularly on the knee and said, 'You peasants drink sherbet the way we swallow medicine.'

Now that the Mayor was joking with him so familiarly, the feeling of inferiority, of being of no consequence, which had invaded Haj Ismail a few moments before was largely dispelled. Was not the Mayor cracking jokes with him? Was this not a good enough reason to feel his self-confidence restored, to feel that the social gap between them was narrowing? He felt pleased. Now it was an appropriate moment for him to start laughing, to pick up the thread of merriment where the Mayor had left off, and thus encourage him to go on in the same vein.

'We peasants cannot tell the sweet flavour of sherbet from the bitter taste of medicine,' he said jestingly.

The Mayor was silent for a moment as though turning the words Haj Ismail had spoken over in his head. He began to feel uneasy. They kept echoing in his ears again and again. Supposing the Mayor misconstrued what he had said?

'Your highness, what I meant is that everything tastes bitter to the mouth of a peasant,' he added hastily in an attempt to set things right.

The Mayor maintained his silence. Decidedly, something was wrong. Haj Ismail was now almost sure that he had not been careful enough about what he had said. This time the Mayor could take his last words to be an insinuation that peasants had a hard life, which of course was not at all true. This in its turn might lead directly or indirectly to an even more dangerous conclusion, namely that in the view of Haj Ismail the government was not telling the truth when it repeatedly expressed its concern for the welfare of the peasants, and the protection of their rights. Since the Mayor was the representative of government in Kafr El Teen, such a view could also be taken to mean that as the responsible official he was using his position to exploit the peasants, and to spend the money he squeezed out of them on his extravagant way of living, and his extravagant tastes in food, tobacco, wine and women.

His mind was now in a whirl. He cursed his own stupidity. 'Instead of painting her lashes with kohl, he had blinded her eyes.'[*]

The best thing to do was to make himself as invisible as he could. But just at that moment he caught a glint in the Mayor's eyes. They were looking in the direction of the river and he turned to see what had caught his attention. High up on the river bank a girl was walking. She held herself upright, balancing the earthenware jar on her head. Her tall figure swayed from side to side, and her large black eyes were raised and carried

---

[*] A popular saying meaning that sometimes when you try to improve a situation you may make it worse.

that expression of pride he had seen so often in the women of Kafrawi's household.

The Mayor moved his head closer to Haj Ismail and said, 'The girl resembles Nefissa.'

Haj Ismail responded quickly. 'She's Nefissa's younger sister.'

'I did not know Nefissa had a sister.'

Haj Ismail realized what was going on in the Mayor's mind, and to curry favour with him said, 'Each one of them is more beautiful than the other.'

The Mayor winked at him and chuckled: 'But the youngest is always the most tasty.'

Haj Ismail laughed loudly sucking in quantities of air through his nose and mouth. He felt in high spirits and was completely rid of the mood of depression which had weighed so heavily on him earlier. Now he was certain that the Mayor's behaviour towards him would not change because his brother was in power. Was he not joking with him as though they were equals, and opening up his heart to him like a friend?

He whispered into the Mayor's ear in hushed tones, blinking his eyes rapidly. 'You are right, your highness, the youngest is always the most savoury to taste.'

The Mayor became very silent. His eyes followed the tall lithe figure of Zeinab as she walked along the river bank. He could see her firm, rounded buttocks pressing up against the long *galabeya* from behind. Her pointed breasts moved up and down with each step. Beneath the tail of her *galabeya* two rosy, rounded heels peeped out.

The Mayor turned round and addressed the Chief of the Village Guard. 'For the life of me I cannot understand how Kafrawi manages to feed these girls of his. Look! The blood is almost bursting out of her heels.'

The Chief of the Village Guard burst into noisy, raucous laughter, gulping in mouthfuls of air. He had suffered a silent torment for quite a while, for it had seemed to him that he was out of favour with the Mayor. Had not the Mayor been talking to Haj Ismail all the time? But now matters looked different. Immediately he felt his mood change, felt himself become gay once more.

'He is stealing from others no doubt. All you have to do is to say the word and we'll push him behind bars.'

He stood up majestically and gave a theatrical wave of his arm. Then pretending to call upon one of his aides, he shouted out loud.

'Boy, bring the handcuffs and chains immediately.'

The Mayor, highly amused by these antics, roared with laughter, and the three men seated with him joined in, including Sheikh Hamzawi who found himself obliged to abandon the water-jar pipe he had been puffing at with zeal all the time, and to laugh more loudly than any of the others, displaying an erratic row of decayed yellow teeth, and jerking the yellow rosary beads frantically between his fingers.

The Mayor waited until the hilarious laughter had subsided before addressing the Chief of the Guard again.

'No, Sheikh Zahran, Kafrawi is not a man to steal.'

Sheikh Hamzawi now found it appropriate to intervene on a categorical note as though he was quoting from the Holy Koran on the sayings of the Prophet Mohamed.

'All peasants steal. Theft runs in their blood like the bilharzia worm. They put on an innocent air, pretend to be dull, kneel down before Allah as they would never think of disobeying Him, but all the time, deep inside, they are nothing but accursed, cunning, unbelieving, impious sons of heretics. A man will prostrate himself in prayer behind me, but once he has left the mosque, and gone to the field, he will steal from his neighbour, or poison the man's buffalo without batting an eyelid.'

He stopped for a moment to cast a look at the Mayor's face. Reassured that his words were falling on appreciative ears, he went on.

'He might even commit murder, or fornication.'

The Chief of the Village Guard crossed his right leg over his left leg, throwing the fold of his garment to one side in a way that exhibited his new pair of boots, and permitted him at the same time to convey the message that Sheikh Hamzawi was trespassing on ground which was strictly his.

'If we are going to speak of murder and fornication then the Chief of the Village Guard should have plenty to say, but...' Turning to the Mayor with an ingratiating smile he asked, 'Tell me, your highness, you who knows so much. Are people in Misr the same as in Kafr El Teen?'

Sheikh Hamzawi intervened unceremoniously. 'People have become corrupt everywhere, Sheikh Zahran,' he said. 'You can search in vain for Islam, or for a devout Muslim. They no longer exist.'

He noticed an expression of disapproval on the Mayor's face and hastily added, 'Except of course where you are dealing with upper class people of noble descent like his highness, the Mayor. Then it's a different matter.'

He searched frantically in his memory for a verse from the Koran with which to back up what he was saying, but his mind had been dulled by the fumes of what he had been smoking. Undeterred, he made do by intoning sanctimoniously, 'Allah enjoins you to inquire after a man's descent for his roots will always find their devious way to his soul.'

The Mayor pouted his fleshy lips at the Sheikh of the mosque. Why had this man led the conversation away from Zeinab's rosy heels to such weighty matters as religion and faith? He smiled in Haj Ismail's direction and said, 'Tell me, in your capacity as doctor-healer in this village, how is it possible that a dark-skinned devil like Kafrawi should have fathered daughters who are as white as a bowl of cream?'

Sheikh Hamzawi butted in again, attempting to chase away the image of the Mayor's disapproving pout, which was still upsetting his tranquillity. He intoned, 'And Allah doth create from the loins of a man of God a corrupt descent.'

'You have not told me what you think, Haj Ismail,' said the Mayor, ignoring Sheikh Hamzawi's interruption.

The village barber was still busy turning over in his mind the title of 'doctor-healer' which the Mayor had bestowed upon him. It made him feel as though he had been accorded a bachelor's degree in medicine, which put him on an equal footing with any medical doctor in the area. He pulled himself up and gazed fixedly in front of him with narrowed eyes as though lost in deep thought. On his face was the look of a man of science, who has penetrated into the secrets of life and is now endowed with great knowledge.

'By Allah, your highness, and verily it is Allah alone who knows, the mother of Nefissa must have been yearning for a bowl of cream at the time when she was pregnant with the girl. Or maybe she was possessed by a white devil.'

The Mayor was seized with a fit of almost uncontrollable laughter. He threw his head back, giving full vent to his mirth, before turning to the Chief of the Village Guard as though looking for someone to come to his rescue.

The Chief of the Village Guard stood up imitating the same

dramatic stance he had adopted a while before, and shouted into the night.

'Boy, bring the handcuffs and chains at once. Catch hold of the devils, boy, and clap them in irons.' Then spitting into the neck of his *galabeya*, he whispered, 'Let not our words anger them, Almighty God.'

Everyone joined in the laughter, but the loudest voice of all was that of Sheikh Hamzawi, who felt that now a special effort was required to melt the ice between him and the Mayor. Leaning over he whispered into his car, 'It's a well-known fact that the womenfolk in the Kafrawi family have their eyes wide open and are quite brazen, your highness.'

The Mayor gurgled softly. 'Is it only their eyes that are wide open, Sheikh Hamzawi?' he asked half seriously.

There was another storm of laughter. It was slowly carried across the still waters of the river, this time sounding carefree, as though the men were at last rid of their bitterness and melancholy. Even the Mayor felt better. He had chased away the bitterness which invaded his heart the moment he saw his brother's picture in the newspaper. Now he no longer had a need to be distracted, or entertained. He yawned copiously, displaying two rows of long white teeth like the fangs of a fox, or a wolf. When he spoke it was in a tone which brooked no discussion.

'Let's go.'

He stood up, and in the wink of an eye the three men were also on their feet.

# III

She piled up pieces of stone and pebbles in the ditch beneath the slope of the river bank, covered them with earth, and flattened the surface with the palm of her hand. Then, resting her arm on the ground, she sat down with her back to the trunk of a mulberry tree. The earth was fresh against her hot skin. A damp coolness seemed to flow from the tree into the aching muscles and bones of her back. She pressed her forehead and face up against it, licking the moisture that exuded from it with her parched tongue.

The moist trunk of the tree evoked an ancient memory, an old sensation. She could almost feel the warm, wet nipple pouring milk into her mouth as she touched it with her lips. A bead of sweat fell from her forehead onto her nose. She wiped it with her sleeve, then her hand moved up to rub her eyes, but they were dry. She whispered softly, 'May Allah have mercy on you my mother.'

She lifted her face to the sky, and the light of dawn shone in her large black eyes. Her eyes had never looked down, nor did she walk with them fixed to the ground. Like her Aunt Zakeya she looked up with pride and with anger, but in her eyes there was no defiance. Over them now lay a cloud of anxiety, as though she was lost and afraid of what lay ahead of her. Her look wandered into the infinite expanses of sky, slowly plunged itself in its depths. In the distance she could see the horizon, a dark line where the earth met the sky. The red disc of the sun climbed out gradually from behind, and started to pour its orange light into the universe. A shiver went through her body. She could not tell whether it was the lingering cold of the night, or the fear of what was yet to come. She lifted her shawl and concealed her face from the light. In front of her the waters of the river were the same as they always had been, and its banks went on and on forever. She looked back, and looking back what she saw seemed no different from what she saw ahead. The same water, and the same track over the river bank stretching out to an endless end. But she knew this time that somewhere in the limitless space was the village she had left behind. And her mind kept remembering things as though she was back, or as though she had never left. The mud hut where she lived, nestling up against her Aunt Zakeya's dwelling. And just in front across the lane that huge gate with the iron bars, shielding the large house which hid behind from curious stares and probing eyes.

She used to crawl on her belly over the dusty lane. If she lifted her head she could see the iron bars like long black legs, watch them advancing slowly, intent on crushing her under their weight. She screamed out in fright, and immediately two strong arms reached out and picked her up. She buried her nose in the black garment. It was homely and rough, and smelt of dough or yeast. When she nestled up against her breast, her mother put something in her mouth. It was a mulberry fruit, ripe and sweet and soft. The tears were still in her eyes but she gulped them down, greedily swallowing the fruit which was filling her mouth with the taste she loved so much.

Ever since childhood the sight of the iron bars had filled her with fright. She heard people mention the gate and the iron bars when they talked of different things. But they never came close, and when they walked through the lane they sidled along the opposite side, and their voices would drop to a whisper the moment it came in sight. The expression in their eyes would change at once from one of pride or anger or even cruelty to a humble resignation as though they had decided to accept anything which fate might do to their lives. They would bow their heads and look at the ground as they passed by, and if one happened to look into their eyes at that moment not even a hint of anger or rebellion could be detected lurking inside.

Once her legs could carry her around she started to go to the fields, either running behind the donkey, or dragging the buffalo by a long rope tied around its neck, to make sure it followed her wherever she went. And every day she carried an earthenware jar on her head, and walked along the river bank to the bend in the Nile where the girls filled up the empty jars with water. But she avoided passing in front of the iron gate, and took a roundabout way behind the village, making almost half a circle to get to the river bank and walk straight down to the filling place. By now she knew that the iron gate opened on the yard which led to the big house owned by the Mayor, and that the house lay far behind, surrounded by a huge garden with trees and flowers. But somehow her imagination kept telling her that behind the gate was concealed a great giant, a monstrous devil who walked on twenty iron legs which could crush her to death at any moment if she was not careful.

When she grew older, instead of taking the roundabout track to the river bank, she started to follow the more direct route, although it led her right in front of the iron gate. She had grown enough to know there were no devils hiding behind it, and that in the big house dwelt the Mayor, his wife and their children. And yet whenever she heard the Mayor being mentioned, a shiver would go through her. Later, when a few more years had passed, the shiver was still there, but now it could barely be sensed deep down inside her.

But one day her father told her that the next morning, as soon as she had dressed and had her breakfast, she was expected to go to the Mayor's house. That night she could not sleep a wink. She was only twelve years old at the time, and her small mind spent the dark hours of the night trying to imagine what the rooms of the Mayor's house could be like. Through it flitted images of a bathroom in white marble which the children of the neighbours had told her about. They added that the Mayor bathed in milk each night. And before her eyes she could see his wife moving around the house, her skin white and smooth, her thighs naked. The son was said to have a room of his own full of guns, and tanks, and aeroplanes which could really fly. The Mayor too kept coming and going before her eyes as real as she had seen him one day swathed in his wide, black cloak, as he walked along surrounded by the men of the village. She remembered now that each time she saw him she used to run away and hide in the house.

In the early morning even before the red light of dawn had appeared in the sky she woke up, washed her hair, rubbed her heels with a stone, put on a clean *galabeya* and a black veil around her hair, and sat down to wait for Sheikh Zahran who was expected to take her to the Mayor's house. But as soon as he came in sight, she ran quickly away and hid on top of the oven. She kept wailing and shrieking from her hiding place, refusing to budge. At one moment she stopped to take her breath, and heard the Chief of the Village Guard say, 'Our Mayor is a generous man, and his wife belongs to a good family. You will be paid twenty piastres a day. You're a stupid girl with no brains. How can you throw away all the good that is coming to you? Do you prefer hunger and poverty rather than doing a bit of work?'

'I work here in my father's house, Sheikh Zahran, and I work in the fields all day,' she answered in a sobbing voice from her hiding place above the oven. 'I am not lazy, but I do not want to go to the Mayor's house.'

The Chief of the Village Guard abandoned his efforts to make her come down and said, 'You people are free to do what you like. It looks as though you are fated not to enjoy all the good which Allah wants to bestow on you. There are hundreds of girls who would jump at a chance to work in the Mayor's house. But he chose your daughter, Kafrawi, because he believes you are a good, honest man worthy of his confidence. What will he say now when he hears you have refused his offer?'

'I am all for accepting, Sheikh Zahran, but as you can see it's the girl who refuses,' answered Kafrawi.

'Then it's the girl who decides what is done in this household, Kafrawi,' exclaimed Sheikh Zahran heatedly.

'No, it's I who decide. But what can I do if she can't see sense?'

'What can you do?! Is that a question for a man to ask?' responded Sheikh Zahran, even more heatedly. 'Beat her. Don't you know that girls and women never do what they're told unless you beat them?'

So Kafrawi called out to her in a firm voice, 'You, Nefissa, come down here at once.'

But Nefissa showed no signs of doing what he told her, so he clambered to the top of the oven, struck her several times, and tugged at her hair until she was obliged to come down. He handed her over to Sheikh Zahran in silence.

To her ears came the sound of wooden wheels turning slowly over the ground. When she turned round she saw a cart pulled by an old tired donkey coming up the track towards her. The donkey suddenly lifted its head and brayed in a long, drawn-out gasping lament. The cart passed in front of her where she sat on the ground. She looked into the eyes of the donkey and saw tears. The man on the seat of the cart was staring at her, so she lifted her shawl to cover her face. His features did not look like anyone she had seen in Kafr El Teen, so she felt more at ease. She called out to him from where she sat on the ground. 'Uncle, please take me with you to Al Ramla,' then stood up on her feet.

The man eyed her where she stood upright on the bank of the river. He noticed her belly was big, and a faint suspicion crept through his mind. But she looked him straight in the face, and her eyes expressed so much anger, and so much pride that his suspicions were allayed. Her movements were slow as though she was spent out, but she held her body upright. His voice sounded gruff when he spoke.

'Get in.'

She rested her arms on the edge of the cart and with a powerful pull lifted herself up to the seat. She sat close to him, her eyes on the road stretched out before them and said nothing. After a short while he gave her belly a quick sidelong glance, then asked, 'Going to your husband in Al Ramla?'

Her eyes did not blink as she said, 'No.'

He was silent for a moment before coming back to the charge again.

'Did you leave your husband behind in Kafr El Teen?'

She kept her eyes on the road and still without blinking said, 'No.'

His looks were becoming more direct. He examined her big, rough hands resting calmly on her lap. The wrists were bare of bracelets. The daughter of some poor peasant, he thought, who is used to digging the ground, and ploughing. Yet when she looked him in the face he saw something he had never noticed before in the eyes of women who belonged to poor peasant families. It was not just anger, nor was it just pride. It was something more powerful than either of them. He suddenly remembered that when still a child he had once climbed up the fence of the Mayor's house. He found himself looking straight into the eyes of the Mayor's daughter. At that moment the stick of the Chief of the Village Guard landed on his shoulders, and he clambered down as fast as he could. Throughout his childhood years he had dreamed of looking into her eyes. He never understood why this desire had taken such a hold on him. He never spoke to anyone about it. It sounded so strange, so mad, so utterly unheard of that he did not dare voice it aloud.

He turned his head and looked at her. Their eyes met and held each other with a steady stare. She neither blinked nor looked away, as any of the girls from Kafr El Teen or Al Ramla would have done in her place. There was an expression in her eyes he could not define. Anger or defiance or maybe both together. So he shifted his gaze to the road, shook the reins over the donkey's back and thought, 'She does not look like someone who has escaped. Nor does she look as though she is afraid.'

His eyes kept wandering back to where she sat. He could see her bare feet covered with cakes of mud which were now drying. He asked again, 'Have you come far?'

With her eyes still fastened on the road she said, 'Yes.'

Still unsatisfied he queried, 'Walking all night?'

'Yes.'

He was silent for some time. He found it difficult to imagine this young woman walking alone through the night over long dusty roads, or cutting through fields where foxes and wolves and brigands lay hidden. But he said nothing for a while, fixing his attention on the road which stretched ahead of them. Then, as though he had turned the matter over in his mind before speaking again, he commented in a low voice, 'The night is dangerous.'

He pronounced the words in a strange, deliberate way as a man would do if he wanted to frighten her, and see the lids of her wide-open eyes tremble in fear. But she continued to stare at the horizon, watching where they were going with unblinking eyes.

'Night is safer than day, uncle,' she said.

He was silent again. The features of his face remained perfectly still like a child whom someone has struck with a stick just a moment ago, but who refuses to show he is hurt, or to burst into tears. He felt a pressure on his chest, like a strong desire to weep kept back for years, ever since the day when the Chief of the Village Guard had whipped him with his cane. If she had turned to him at this moment and smiled, he would have rested his head on her breast, and wept like a child. Or if he had seen the slightest quiver in her eyes when he gazed into them as the cart started to rock from side to side he might have enjoyed a sense of relief for a while. But she did not quiver and she did not smile.

She did not even turn to look at him as though she had forgotten his presence by her side. Even at the rare moments when she did, he felt she was thinking of something else, so important, so big that by comparison he remained as of little consequence as the droppings of a fly. He dipped a hand into his pocket and pulled out a plug of molassed tobacco, or maybe it was a piece of hashish, or opium. He put it in his mouth. His saliva tasted bitter and he swallowed several times, then started to cough violently as though trying to overcome an age-long feeling of humiliation he carried deep down inside him. He bent his head with the deep sadness of a man who has just realized that the only real feeling he has known is this sense of humiliation that he carries around with him, day after day, and night after night.

He closed his lips tightly, and whipped the old donkey several times with the long stick he held in his hand, just as the Chief of the Village Guard would do with the child of poor parents caught playing after school. Now he felt in a hurry to reach Al Ramla, and to be rid of this irksome young woman as soon as he could.

The wooden cart advanced slowly over the winding road, swaying from side to side so much that it looked as though at any moment a wheel might come off. She could hear the donkey gasping and choking as it went along. His breathing sounded slow and monotonous like a clock, like the bumping of the wooden cart wheels as they turned round and round, and the pulse beating under her ribs and inside her belly as though it too was on the verge of breaking down.

She watched the sun rise up into the sky. She watched the fields swing slowly behind, and the compact mass of mud huts emerge from the ground and huddle up against the bank of the river like a mound of earth piled up on one side. Gradually women carrying water jars came in sight as they walked along the river bank moving towards her in a leisurely line. She began to hear a buzzing noise filling the air, for the children had awakened and the flies swarmed through the alleys and over the houses. Long queues of buffalo and cows plodded along raising clouds of dust, and groups of men and women walked by their side. They carried hoes on their shoulders and kept yawning all the time as though the thought that another day was about to start made them wearier than ever.

For a moment it seemed to her that she was back where she had started out, back in Kafr El Teen. She lifted her veil to hide her face but the man sitting beside her spoke to her in a hoarse, ugly voice which said, 'Get down.'

'Is this Al Ramla, uncle?' she asked.

'Yes,' he said without looking at her.

She rested her arms on the wooden cart and started to get down. It leaned suddenly on one side under the weight of her body and straightened up again when her feet reached the ground. The cart regained its balance and he felt it become light, moving more easily over the ground. His heart was beating steadily and he would feel that now it was much lighter than it was before, as though rid of the load which had been weighing it down. He heard her footsteps tread heavily over the ground and whipped the donkey with his stick several times. The cart resumed its slow progress, trundling along over the dusty road. He was on the verge of turning round to take a last look at her, but changed his mind. He fastened his eyes on the distant horizon and whipped the donkey again. It stumbled forwards gasping for breath as it dragged the cart behind it, and the wheels started to turn once more with their slow, monotonous, bumping sound.

Nefissa saw the cart shaking and swaying from side to side, the man's back was thin, and his bones stuck out, and when she looked at him from behind she was reminded of her father. After a while the cart disappeared carrying the man out of sight, but the sound of the wheels crunching over the ground continued to mingle in her ears with the hoarse gasping of the donkey as it breathed in and out. Every now and then these sounds were drowned in a rasping cough like the cough which shook her father every time he inhaled deeply from his water-jar pipe as he sat smoking in the yard of their house.

When she arrived at the mosque she turned to the right and after a short distance was confronted by an area of waste ground which Om Saber had described to her. At the furthest end was a small house built of mud, with a big wooden door. Over the door was a wooden knocker, and close by she noticed the water pump. She worked the pump and drank the water which flowed over the palm of her hand, then walked up to the door. She lifted the knocker several times, allowing it to drop lightly, and heard a woman's voice respond in a long, drawn-out vulgar call like that of Nafoussa, the dancer in Kafr El Teen.

'Who is at the door?'

'It's me,' answered Nefissa in what was little more than a whisper.

The long, drawn-out vulgar call resounded loudly once more. 'Who are you?'

'It's me... Nefissa,' she said.

'Nefissa who?' the woman insisted.

She wiped a drop of sweat which was trickling down her nose and said, 'Aunt, Om Saber sent me to you, Aunt Nafoussa.'

There was a silence. She could hear the pounding of her heart, and the whisper of her breath as she faced the door.

Then it swung open by itself, as though moved by an invisible devil.

She stood there as still as a statue. But when she stepped across the threshold she realized that her whole body was shivering.

# IV

Just before she heard the first cock crow in the dark silence, Fatheya opened her eyes. Or perhaps she did not realize that her eyes had already been open for some time. She could see her husband lying on his back with his mouth open, snoring with a deep choking noise. His breath smelt heavily of tobacco, and his chest kept up a wheezing sound as though phlegm had been collecting in it all night.

She nudged him in the shoulder with her fist to wake him up, but he turned over and gave his back to her, muttering unintelligible words in his slumber. The crow of the cock rang out in the silence once more. This time she hit him with her knuckles sharply on the shoulder.

'Sheikh Hamzawi, the cock has awakened and called out to prayer, and you are still snoring away,' she said irritably.

Sheikh Hamzawi opened his eyes but closed his lips tightly as though he had decided not to respond to her verbal and manual attacks on him, already starting at this early hour of the day. He got up without a word. His wife, Fatheya, was not like his previous wives. None of them would ever have dared to look him straight in the face, or to say anything inappropriate to him, or compare him to any other man in Kafr El Teen, let alone to a cock which had crowed a few moments earlier, and which she had had the impudence to insinuate was better than he.

But he no longer cared how she behaved, even if it went as far as putting the cock on an equal level with him. What mattered was that he had succeeded in forcing her to marry him against her will, and obliging her to live with him all these years even though Haj Ismail's potions and amulets had been totally ineffective in restoring or even patching up his virility.

The first time he had seen her, he was seated as usual in front of Haj Ismail's shop. He glimpsed her supple body as she walked along the river bank carrying an earthenware jar on her head. Turning to Haj Ismail, he had whispered, 'That girl over there. Who's she?'

'Fatheya, the daughter of Masoud,' answered Haj Ismail.

'Her father is that poor man then. No doubt he would be happy to have me as a member of the family?'

'Do you mean that you want to marry her, Sheikh Hamzawi?'

'Why not? I have been married three times and still have no son. I must have a son before I die.'

'But she is young enough to be one of your grandchildren,' said Haj Ismail. 'Besides, how do you know that she will not remain childless like your previous wives?'

Sheikh Hamzawi bowed his head to the ground in silence, but the rosary beads continued to run uninterruptedly through his fingers, impelled by a mechanism of their own. Haj Ismail eyed him with a knowing smile. He burst into a laugh, cut it short abruptly and said, 'It looks as though the girl has turned your head for you, Sheikh Hamzawi.'

Sheikh Hamzawi smiled quietly and looked at the village barber with a gleam in his eyes. 'Verily the look of her revives my spirit. I've always longed for the kind of female she is.'

'Talking of females, female she certainly is. Her eyes seethe with desire. But do you think you can keep her under control, Sheikh Hamzawi? Do you think a man of your age can take her on?'

'I can satisfy not only her, but her father if necessary,' retorted Sheikh Hamzawi. 'It's only what you have in your pocket that counts where a man is concerned.'

'What will you do if the years go by and she does not give you a son?' enquired Haj Ismail.

'Allah is great, Haj Ismail. I am going through difficult times, but they will soon be over. God will breathe his spirit into me, and give me strength.'

Haj Ismail laughed out loudly. 'Those are the kind of things you can say to other people, but not to me, Sheikh Hamzawi. You haven't stopped complaining to me about your condition. How can Allah give you strength? Are you insinuating that God will...?'

Sheikh Hamzawi cut him short quickly. 'Allah can infuse life into dead bones, Haj Ismail. Besides you yourself told me that I can be cured.'

'But you have not been listening to my advice, nor have you followed the treatment I prescribed to you. You've been lending an attentive ear to what the doctors say, and paying through your eyes for their medicines. I told you, doctors know nothing and their prescriptions are useless. But you did not believe me. And now what is the result? You've wasted your money and you're not one step ahead of where you were. Say so, if I'm wrong.'

'Yes, yes, Haj Ismail, but one cannot learn except at a high price. Now I know all doctors are ignorant cheats, and that the only real doctor in the village is you. From now on I refuse to be treated by anyone else. But you must marry me to Fatheya, the daughter of Masoud. If you do that, Allah will reward you generously, because you will have done a service to the man who preserves the holy mosque and defends the teachings of God in this village.'

Haj Ismail burst into hilarious laughter. 'Both I and my children would have died of hunger long ago if we had waited until Allah rewards us.'

'Of course I will pay you, and handsomely. You know me well,' Sheikh Hamzawi said quickly.

'I know you are a generous man, and that you are the descendant of a generous family. But most important of all, you are the man who preserves the faith in this village and watches over our morals. Therefore you must leave the matter in the hands of Allah, and not worry about it any further. I will see to it. You can depend on that. Just follow what I told you to do before. Make constant use of warm water, and salt, and lemon. Burn your incense every night leaving none of it to the following morning, then take the rosary between your fingers and recite a thanksgiving to Allah ninety-nine times. After that, curse your first wife thirty-three times, for were you not fully potent when you married her, Sheikh Hamzawi?'

Sheikh Hamzawi answered in a voice that rang with despair, 'I was as strong as a horse.'

'She managed to cast a spell on you, and I know who prepared the amulet for her. He is not from Kafr El Teen, but I know the secret of his spell, and how to destroy it. The most important thing for you now is to follow my advice, and Allah will bestow his blessings upon you.'

Sheikh Hamzawi lowered his voice to a barely audible whisper and asked, 'When will I spend the betrothal night with Fatheya?'

'Soon, very soon, if Allah wills.'

'What about my having a son, Haj Ismail? I suppose it is impossible?'

'Nothing is impossible if Allah wills that it should not be so. You are a man of God and should know that well. How can you forget that Allah is all powerful?'

The rosary beads ran quickly between the fingers of Sheikh Hamzawi and he gasped, 'May His name be praised. May His name be praised.'

Sheikh Hamzawi rested his hand on the wall and slowly got to his feet. The rosary swayed from side to side in his hand as he repeated 'May His name be praised.' He put on his caftan and his *jiba*, and adjusted the turban on his head, all the time whispering under his breath. His thin body seemed to bow under a heavy weight as he shuffled towards the door of the house. He heard Fatheya moan in a low voice. He could not understand what was wrong with her these days. She was not the same. She did not even get angry with him as she used to do at one time, and spent most of her day in the house lying down. She no longer insisted on visiting her aunt, perhaps because each time he got into a temper and tried to stop her from going out. The wife of Sheikh Hamzawi, as he had explained to her father, was not like the wives of other men. Her husband was responsible for upholding the teachings of Allah, and keeping the morals and piety of the village intact. The wife of a man like that was not supposed to be seen by just anyone. Her body had to be concealed even from her closest relatives, except for her face and the palms of her hands. She was expected to live in his house surrounded by all due care and respect, never to be seen elsewhere except twice in her life. The first time when she moved from her father's to her husband's house. And the second when she left her husband's house for the grave allotted to her in the burial grounds. Apart from that …

The father shook his head in pious agreement and said, 'Sheikh Hamzawi, you are indeed the most respected and esteemed of all men,' then he gave his consent.

But Fatheya hid herself above the oven and refused to answer anyone, despite all the efforts expended to make her more reasonable.

'God is going to save you from the withering sun in the fields, from the dirt and the dung, from your diet of dry bread and salted pickles. Instead you will spend your days resting in the shade, eating white bread and meat. You will become the spouse of Sheikh Hamzawi, the man who devotes himself to the worship of God, to serving his mosque, the man who leads the people of the village in prayer, and lives a life of piety,' said Haj Ismail at the top of his voice, as though he wanted everyone within hearing distance to know what was going on.

But Fatheya continued to hide on top of the oven and refused to answer.

Haj Ismail looked round at her father and inquired in angry tones, 'Now what do we do, Masoud?'

'You can see, Haj Ismail, the girl is refusing.'

'Do you mean that in your household it's the girl who decides what should be done?'

'But what can I do?' asked the father looking perplexed.

'What do you do?' exclaimed Haj Ismail, now looking furious. 'Is that a question for a man to ask? Beat her, my brother, beat her once and twice and thrice. Do you not know that girls and women are only convinced if they receive a good hiding?'

Masoud remained silent for a moment, then he called out, 'Fatheya, come here at once.'

But there was no answer, so he climbed up on to the top of the oven, pulled her out by her hair, and beat her several times until she came down. Then he handed her over to Haj Ismail and the same day she married the pious old Sheikh.

Sheikh Hamzawi grasped his stick firmly in his hand, and opened the door of his house. Fatheya strained her ears to catch the tapping sound of his stick through the wall as he walked on its outer side. She knew the sound well. It had continued to echo in her ears ever since the night of her betrothal. It pierced through the thick shawl wrapped around her body and head as she rode the donkey to Sheikh Hamzawi's house. She could hear its tap, tap, tap as he walked along the lane by her side. Her father wore a new *galabeya* and Om Saber, the *daya*, was clad in a long, black dress. She could not see the old woman for the folds of the shawl were worn tightly round her head. She could not see anything.

But she felt. She felt the burning pain left by the woman's finger as it probed up between her thighs looking for blood. And she felt the warm gush and the sticky wet. She did not see the clean white towel stained red, nor the wound the woman's nail had made in her flesh. But she felt her virgin colours had bled, for in her ears resounded the beat of the drums, the shrieks of joy and the high-pitched trilling of the women.

She moved her hand in under the shawl and wiped the sweat from her nose and eyes, but it continued to pour out from the roots of her hair down over her face and her neck to her chest and her back. Underneath her, on the back of the donkey its rough coat was becoming wetter and wetter. The spine of the donkey pressed up between her thighs. She could feel it hard against the wound which was still bleeding inside. With every step, with every beat of the *tabla*, the back of the donkey rose and fell, and its thin spine moved up and down to rub on her wounds, causing her a sharp pain every time, and making her lips open in a noiseless cry. The warm blood trickled out mixing with the sweat which poured down from her body, and the rough coat of the donkey felt soaking wet between her thighs.

When they arrived in front of the house which belonged to the pious and God-fearing man who had become her spouse, they took her down from the donkey, but she was unable to stand on her feet, and collapsed into the arms of those who stood around, to be carried into the house like a sack of cotton.

She realized she had left the streets and was now in the house from the dank, putrid smell of the air inside. Since she was sure that the odour of godliness and moral uprightness smelt good and was pleasant to respire, she realized her nose was to blame for making the atmosphere around her smell like a latrine which was never washed down. She did not know exactly what it was that was wrong with her, but ever since her childhood she had felt there was something impure about her, that something in her body was unclean and bad. Then one day Om Saber came to their house, and she was told that the old woman was going to cut the bad, unclean part off. She was overcome by a feeling of overwhelming happiness. She was only six years old at the time.

After having done what she was supposed to do, Om Saber went away leaving a small wound between her thighs. It continued to bleed for several days. But even after it healed she was still left with something unclean in her body which used to bleed for several days at a time. Each time she had her periods the people around her would have a changed expression in their eyes when they looked at her, or they would avoid her as though there was something corrupt or bad about her.

Later, when she married Sheikh Hamzawi, he too would shy away from her whenever she had her periods, and treat her as though she was a leper. If his hand inadvertently touched her shoulder, or her arm, he would exhort Allah to protect him from the evil Satan. Then he would go to the water closet, wash himself five times and do his ablutions again if he had already done them. In addition she was not allowed to read the Koran or to listen to it being read or recited. But once her periods were over, and she had taken a bath, and cleansed herself thoroughly, he allowed her to pray, and to recite passages from the Koran.

Every night before she went to bed Sheikh Hamzawi made her sit on a carpet opposite him, and showed her how to pray. She did not understand what the words he recited meant, they were difficult words and she kept asking him to explain their meaning to her. But he used to respond in a very discouraging and rough way, insisting that the words of Allah and the rituals of prayer were supposed to be learnt by heart and not understood. So Fatheya tried to memorize them as best she could. The instructions of Sheikh Hamzawi kept echoing in her ears.

'Prayer is built on certain well defined movements of the body, namely: kneeling, prostrating yourself twice each time you kneel, and then sitting up with your feet under the body to recite the testimonial. In addition, there are certain conditions which must be strictly adhered to. In males the body must be covered from the waist downwards to a point below the knees. In females, the whole body should be covered with the exception of the palms of the hands, and the face. At the beginning of the prayer you must stand upright with the face looking straight in front of you, and the feet kept straight on the ground. In the case of males the hands should be lifted and held in line with the ears when declaiming the All Powerfulness and Almightiness of Allah. In females the hands should be held in line with the shoulder bone. The next movement in males is to put the right hand over the left hand and cover the belly below the waist with both the hands, whereas in females the hands are to be placed over the chest.

'Whenever you kneel or prostrate yourself you must do it completely. When you kneel repeat, "I praise thee O Almighty God" three times. And when you prostrate yourself repeat, "I praise thee O highest of all gods" three times. Your prayers become null and void if you say anything extraneous to the words of the prayer, or laugh or soil your cleanliness after ablutions in any way, particularly if you let out wind from the back passage.'

So every evening Fatheya would sit on the prayer carpet and repeat the same ritual. Then she would recite the holy verse of 'The Seat', and perhaps other verses. Her lids would feel heavy, and quite often she fell asleep while kneeling. In het ears echoed the words of Allah and between her thighs crept the hand of Sheikh Hamzawi. She abandoned herself to sleep as though abandoning herself to a man, opening her thighs wide apart and dropping into a deep oblivion right in the middle of the prayer offered to God.

With her ear stuck to the wall, Fatheya followed the tapping noise made by Sheikh Hamzawi's stick as he moved along the lane. She could detect the sound of his foot if it collided with anything on the ground. His eyesight was weak and his stick or his foot seemed always to be colliding with something, or getting entangled in it. It could be a dead rabbit, or a dead cat, or a stone, or a pebble which he would strike away from the door with a sweep of his stick. Sometimes his foot got entangled in his caftan as he stepped over the threshold of his house, making him falter, or his shoe would land on a clod of manure, or the droppings which a dog had left in front of the door since the night before. The rosary would sway furiously in his hand as he heaped curses over dogs and people alike.

But this time his foot collided with a body that was neither that of a dead rabbit, nor of a dead cat. It was moving, and alive, and also much bigger. He was seized with fright thinking it could be a spirit, or an elf of the night. But a moment later he heard a faint moaning, and when he looked down at the ground despite his dimmed eyesight, he could discern what looked like a rosy face, two eyes with tears at the fringes of the closed lashes, and an open mouth with lips which trembled slightly, as it breathed in air with a gasping sound.

For a moment he stood stock still not daring to move. Could it be that Allah had responded to his prayers? Had the amulet of Haj Ismail at last produced its magic effect? This child seemed as though it had fallen from the night sky right in front of his door, just as Christ had come down from on high to where the Virgin Mary had lain down to rest under a tree.

His lips opened to emit a faint choking sound. Nothing was beyond the power of Allah, praised be His name, and clamoured to the high heavens. He continued to stand as still as a statue. His long, narrow face looked even longer than usual, but now it started to show up more distinctly as the pale light of dawn touched it. His eyes were slightly misty, and over one of them was a white spot which shone mysteriously. The yellow beads of his rosary were worn away where his fingers had rubbed against them during the endless hours of a lifetime spent in worship and prayer. But now, maybe for the first time during his waking hours, the beads had ceased to go round.

At that precise moment of the new day the Chief of the Village Guard had ended his night vigil and was on his way home. He came upon the figure of Sheikh Hamzawi standing motionless in front of his door. He had never seen him standing like that before, nor ever seen his face look so long and drawn. It was as though he now had two faces. The upper one was that of Sheikh Hamzawi, whereas the lower face bore no resemblance to him at all, nor to any other face he had seen in Kafr El Teen, nor for that matter, in the whole wide world, although he had not seen much of what was outside Kafr El Teen. It resembled neither the face of a human being, nor that of a spirit. For all he knew it could have been the face of a devil, or that of a saint, or even the face of God himself, except that he knew not what the face of God looked like, since it was not a face that he had seen.

He halted suddenly, and stood there as though turned to stone. His eyes were fixed on the strange ghostlike form the like of which he had never set his eyes on before. For it was not like man, or saint, or devil, or any other of the many creations of God. He saw it bend and lift something that lay at its feet. He felt his fingers close tightly around the huge stick he carried around with the instinctive movement of the village guard. He was on the point of lifting it high up in the air to bring it down with all his might on the head bending low over the ground. But at that very moment he caught sight of a rosy face with traces of tears peeping through the closed eyes, and he heard Sheikh Hamzawi's voice intone, 'Without God we are indeed hapless for without Him we can do nothing.'

'What is this, Sheikh Hamzawi?' exclaimed the Chief of the Village Guard in a loud voice.

'An angel from heaven,' muttered Sheikh Hamzawi.

'And why could it not be a devil, son of a devil?' said the Chief of the Village Guard.

Still almost unaware of what was going on, Sheikh Hamzawi replied, 'It's a gift from Allah.'

Before he had time to finish his sentence, Fatheya had poked her head through the door. 'Say not what you are saying, Sheikh Zahran,' she said in a voice full of anger. 'It is a gift, a blessing from Allah. Only that which is sinful should be condemned.'

She stretched out her arms and rapidly snatched the child from Sheikh Hamzawi who was still standing in the same place, looking as though he did not know what was going on. She closed the door holding the child closely to her bosom. She could feel her breasts tingle as the blood flowed through them, like tiny ants moving deeply in her flesh. She pulled her breast out through the open neck of her garment and pressed the nipple, letting white drops of milk ooze out of the little dark opening. She wrapped her shawl carefully around the head of the baby, before slipping her nipple into its greedy, gasping mouth.

# V

The voice of Sheikh Hamzawi soared into the air as the almost invisible glimmer of dawn crept through the sky. It floated over the low mud huts, pierced through the dark walls, dropped down into the narrow winding lanes blocked with scattered mounds of manure, to reach the ears of the Chief of the Village Guard who was now sitting in his house. But this time he had not undressed as he was in the habit of doing the moment he got back from his long night vigil. Nor did he ask his wife to bring him something to eat. He did not even take off his leather boots with the usual quick movement followed by two successive kicks which sent them flying into a corner of the room, as though he was ridding himself of a heavy chain wound around his feet.

He reclined on the mat, his eyes wide open, staring at nothing, his boots securely attached round his ankles. His fingers kept pulling at his long thick whiskers as he was wont to do when he had come upon a dead body lying in some field, or on the river bank, but did not yet know who was the killer, or when a crime had been committed behind his back without his knowing right from the start how the whole thing had been planned.

When the voice of Sheikh Hamzawi went through the village to where he sat, he turned his head and looked at his wife. His lips parted slightly as though he was about to tell her that something important had happened in Kafr El Teen that night. But his wife was quicker to it this time. 'Nefissa, Kafrawi's daughter, has run away,' she said, pronouncing the sentence quickly, almost in one breath, with a jerk of her hand which resembled the kick her husband gave with his foot when he wanted to rid himself of his heavy boots. The news had been whispered to her by one of her neighbours the night before. She spent the long, dark hours tossing and turning on her bed. It seemed to weigh down on her chest with a palpable mass of its own. It oppressed her, and yet carried with it an obscure pleasure, like being pregnant and waiting for the dawn in eager anticipation, for the moment when she could shift this weight to someone else, and enjoy the thrill of telling her man the news that Nefissa had fled before he was told about it by anyone apart from herself.

The name Nefissa rang with a strange sound in the ears of Sheikh Zahran. The image of a small, rosy face with closed eyes and still wet tears around the lids floated in space. For a moment the closed lids opened wide, and he looked into the girl's big black eyes – as they stared straight ahead at something on the distant horizon. His fingers let go of his whiskers, and he gave a sudden gasp like a drowning man when he comes to the surface. His voice rang out.

'Nefissa?'

'Yes, Nefissa,' she said.

Fatheya still sat huddled up close to the wall, with the baby held close to her chest. Its head was swathed in her dark veil, and its lips suckled at the nipple of her breast. If she had not kept her ear to the wall she might not have heard it vibrate with the name Nefissa. She gave a sudden gasp of relief like a drowning woman who unexpectedly finds herself at the surface.

'Nefissa?'

The name Nefissa echoed in the dark rooms, pierced through the walls of mud, crept through the lanes blocked with piles of manure, rose into the air over the low irregular roofs covered in cakes of dung and cotton sticks, higher and higher over the minaret of the mosque and the crescent at its top. Before long it was pounding at the high brick walls and the iron door of the Mayor's house. It resounded in his ears like the summons to prayer tolled out five times a day by Sheikh Hamzawi from the highest point in the village of Kafr El Teen, lying like some dark fungus by the waters of the Nile.

Seated next to the Mayor was his youngest son Tariq. He had just entered college and had come down to the village for his holidays. As he listened to her story his eyes shone with the glint which can be seen in the eyes of a youth barely nineteen when he thinks of a woman's body, with the relief which can come from images and words when the act itself is forbidden. His voice was husky when he said, 'Last week in college we discovered a child in the water closet. And the week before we caught a couple kissing in an empty lecture room. Now here in Kafr El Teen a girl gives birth to her child, abandons it in front of the house of the village Sheikh, and runs away. Girls have no morals these days, father.'

'Yes, son, you are quite right,' the Mayor answered. 'Girls and women have lost all morality.' He accompanied his words with a quick sidelong glance which lingered for a moment on the bare thighs of his wife showing beneath her tight skirt. She crossed one leg over the other with a barely contained irritation, and commented heatedly, 'Why not admit that it's men who no longer have any morals?'

The Mayor laughed. 'There's nothing new to that. Men have always been immoral. But now the women are throwing virtue overboard, and that will lead to a real catastrophe.'

'Why a catastrophe? Why not equality, or justice?'

The son shook his long-haired, curly head, and gave his mother a reproving look.

'No, mother, I don't agree with you when you talk of equality. Girls are not the same as boys. The most precious thing they possess is their virtue.'

The Mayor's wife burst into soft peals of sarcastic, slightly snorting laughter evocative of the more vulgar mirth that could be expressed by the lady patron of a brothel if she had been involved in the conversation. She raised one eyebrow and said, 'Is that so, Master Tariq. Now you are putting on a Sheikh's turban and talking of virtue. Where was your virtue hiding last week when you stole a ten pound note from my handbag, and went to visit that woman with whose house I have now become quite familiar? Where was your virtue last year when you assaulted Saadia, the servant, and obliged me to throw her out in order to avoid a scandal? And where does your virtue disappear to every time you pounce on one of the servant girls in our house? Matters have gone so far that I have now decided to employ only menservants. Pray tell me what happens to your virtue when you are so occupied pursuing the girls on the telephone, or across windows, or standing on our balconies, or don't you know that our neighbours in Maadi have complained to me several times?'

She directed her words to her son, but kept throwing looks of barely disguised anger towards the Mayor. The rigid features of his face convinced the boy that the usual quarrel was about to break out between them, so he quickly switched back to the story of Nefissa.

'Father, do you think Sheikh Hamzawi will adopt the child?'

'It looks as though he intends to do so,' said the Mayor. 'He's a good man and has no children. His wife has been wanting to have a baby for years.'

'Then the problem is solved,' said the son with an air of finality.

'It's not solved at all. These peasants never calm down unless they wreak vengeance on whoever is the cause,' chimed in the mother.

After this parting shot she stood up and went off to her room. The son did not notice the small muscle which had started to quiver below his father's mouth. He pretended he was scratching his chin or playing with an old pimple in order to hide its nervous twitch. His blue eyes wandered away, as though his thoughts had become occupied with something else. After a prolonged silence he said, 'I wonder who the man could be? And whether he's from Kafr El Teen? Which he most probably is. However, he might easily have come from somewhere else.'

'People like Nefissa know nothing outside Kafr El Teen,' commented the boy.

'Why do you say that?'

'Well, you know these peasant girls. They're so simple.'

'I don't think Nefissa was that simple. I've never seen a girl whose look was so brazen.'

'Yes, she was a rather forward girl, and the man must have been pretty rash himself.'

The Mayor said hastily, 'That's why I'm inclined to think that he's not from Kafr El Teen. I know all the men here, and I don't think there's a single one of them who has any guts, let alone the guts to do a thing like that. Don't you agree with me, Tariq?'

Tariq was silent for a moment. The faces of the men he knew in Kafr El Teen started to parade before his eyes. He heard his father say, 'Could you guess who it might be?'

The faces continued to float along before his eyes. Suddenly a face stood out in front, absolutely immobile. Or perhaps it was his eyes which had singled out this face from among the many faces that went by. He examined its features with growing curiosity. And a voice within him began to say 'Elwau.' He did not know why in the midst of all the faces he had seen at one time or another, this face in particular imposed itself upon him. He had never seen Elwau and Nefissa together. Elwau dwelt at the eastern outskirts of the village, whereas Nefissa lived near the opposite limits on the west. But no sooner did he try to think seriously of a man who could plausibly be linked to Nefissa's life than the face of Elwau surged up from somewhere inside his mind. He had never met him face-to-face except once. Now and again he would glimpse him at a distance walking along with his hoe on his shoulder. He was always silent, never spoke to anyone, or turned his head to look at a shop, or a house. Nor was he ever the first to call out a greeting to those whom he crossed on his way, even if it was the Chief of the Village Guard, or the Sheikh of the mosque, or even the Mayor himself.

No one could say that he had been seen with Nefissa or with any other of the women of Kafr El Teen. But every day he could be seen ploughing his field, or digging the soil with his hoe. Even on Fridays, when everybody went to the mosque, to stand behind Sheikh Hamzawi while he led the village in prayer, he would be at work in the field. After sunset he sat on the bank of the river watching its waters flow by, or gazing at the trees standing erect against the horizon. If somebody passed by, he did not look round, and if a person proffered him the usual greeting, his quiet voice rang out in the silence with the words of Salam, but his body continued to sit immobile.

The lips of the boy's mouth moved slightly to pronounce the name Elwau. Yet if anyone had happened to ask him why of all the names he knew in the village that of Elwau in particular had occurred to him at the time, it is doubtful if he could have been able to find an answer. He had met him face-to-face only once. But that one time, it seems, must have been enough for him to see his eyes. And to see his eyes must have been enough for him to realize that they were not the same as the other men's eyes. They were not fixed on the ground, but looked straight ahead of him with the expression of pride, which could also be seen in Nefissa's eyes. He remembered that day now. In what was probably no more than the fraction of a second was born in his mind a link, nay, an unforgettable tie, between what he had seen in their eyes. He could not define what it was exactly, but he knew without a doubt that it was there, deep inside. And it remained with him long after the memory of his encounters with them had sunk into the dark, forgotten recesses of his mind.

But the moment the face of Elwau emerged before his eyes he understood how certain things could never fade away, never die, even if they were no bigger than a drop of water in the ocean, or lasted no longer than a short moment in the infinity of time. So when his father repeated the question he heard a voice within him say 'Elwau.'

And his eyes opened wide with surprise when his father re-iterated, 'Elwau?' for he had not yet had the time to open his lips and pronounce the name 'Elwau' or at least so it seemed to him, as he sat there turning things over in his mind. Yet as soon as his father echoed the name, the face he had seen only once before emerged from dark into light, changed from a hazy memory, to a reality in life. His voice rose up from his depths and vibrated with an audible sound in the air outside.

'Elwau?!' it said.

The Mayor pronounced the name again as though to ensure that this time it was transformed into indelible fact.

'Elwau,' he said.

The iron gate opened wide to let in three men. Sheikh Hamzawi, Sheikh Zahran, and Haj Ismail. They filed in, one behind the other, and walked up to where the Mayor sat. No one knows whether they heard him pronounce the name of the man, but they repeated in one breath, 'Elwau.' Their voices echoed in the yard around the house, climbed over the high wall of red brick, cut into the dark mud huts to be repeated in the households before they lighted the kerosene lamps, leapt over the roofs and dropped into the twisting lanes and alleys, creeping along everywhere before the sun had yet had the time to set and light the other side of the earth's globe.

Tariq leaned over the balustrade. Below the terrace the waters of the Nile were crimson red. He watched the sun drop below the distant horizon, and the children playing on the river bank. He could hear them chanting as they wove a ragged line and danced. and clapped.

Camel driver, camel driver,
It's Nefissa and Elwau
Nefissa, Nefissa, Elwau is in the basket
Elwau, Elwau, Nefissa is in the field
Camel driver, camel driver
It's Nefissa and Elwau...

His eyes opened wide in amazement, as though he could hardly believe his ears. He turned to his mother who was standing by his side, and almost breathless with surprise, asked in a halting voice, 'Mother, is it really Elwau?'

'How should I know?' she replied in a voice full of irritation. 'Why don't you ask your father, the Mayor?'

# VI

It was a Friday; the burning disc of the sun like a ball of fire in the centre of the sky, glared down on Kafrawi's head. His eyes seemed to be bathed in the red colour of the sun's rays, and the sweat poured out of him from every pore, streaming down his head, his neck, his chest, his belly and his thighs. He could feel it warm and sticky as it slid over his thighs to his legs, down to the cracked, horny skin of his bare feet. He felt wet as though he had urinated on himself. He slipped his hand under his *galabeya* and touched himself. He could not tell the difference between the feel of his sweat and his urine, nor could he sense whether his muscles were relaxed, or contracted, still or moving. All he knew was that he seemed to have lost all control over his arms and his legs. His body had become a separate part of him, a huge muscle which contracted or relaxed of its own accord, moved or kept still as he stood there watching it, so that he could hardly believe what was happening under his own eyes to this body of his which had always been a part of him. It was as though his soul had left his body and hovered at a distance, or as though another soul which was not his had slipped into his body.

When he saw his bare feet covered in their dry, cracked skin walk out of the field, he wondered at what was happening with amazement. How could his legs walk out of the field like this on their own? He tried to muster enough strength in order to stop them, and for a moment he thought he had succeeded, but they continued to stride slowly out of the field, and out of his control to the only place where the burning rays of the sun could not reach him at that time of the day – to the stable.

It was not really a stable. It was just a shed made of bamboo cane, palm tree fronds and maize stalks, plastered over with mud to form four walls and a roof. The buffalo would lie under it during the summer days and during the winter Kafrawi would spend some of his nights sheltered by its walls.

The buffalo was lying on her belly as she usually did when the weather was hot. Her large, brooding eyes gazed at the dark mud wall, and her jaws moved slowly churning something invisible over and over again, while fine white bubbles of saliva kept coming and going at the corners of her mouth every time she breathed out or in.

Kafrawi's body dropped down on the ground close to where she lay. His eyes fastened themselves on something with the same silent, brooding look. He tried to contract the muscles of his lids and close his eyes in an attempt at sleep. But they remained wide open, continuing to stare fixedly at the dark wall of mud. The buffalo looked at him. Her big eyes were covered in a film of moisture, like tears that had not yet formed. She stretched out her neck coming so close that their heads touched. Then she started to wipe her lips up against his neck like a mother fondling her child. It seemed as though she was trying to say something to him, to ask him what was wrong. He rested his head on hers, wiped his wet eyes over her face, and brought his parched lips close up to her ear. He whispered, 'O, Aziza, Nefissa is no longer here. She has run away.'

And so Kafrawi started to speak to the buffalo, to tell her what had happened. She seemed to answer him, and somehow he could understand what she said. For ever since he had opened his eyes and taken his first look at the world around him, the buffalo had been somewhere close by, either in the field or in the house. Before he learnt to walk, or to pronounce his first words he could see her looking at him with her big, silent eyes as he stood alone in some dark corner crying bitterly as only children know how to cry.

When he began to crawl on his belly over the ground, the first thing he started to do was to crawl in her direction. He could feel her touch his face with her smooth lips. Somehow she could tell when his lips were parched and dry. She would move gradually towards him until her nipple was close to his mouth, and when he opened his eyes he could see the swollen udder with the black nipple hanging down. The smell of her milk floated around him, made him stretch his neck and close his lips over it tightly, and almost immediately he would feel the warm flow of milk in his mouth.

As soon as he could pronounce a few words he called out to her. He named her Aziza, and whenever she heard the name she would turn her head towards him, and her eyes would say 'Yes, Kafrawi.' Every day he pronounced a new word, and she answered with a look in her eyes which said something different each time. Gradually they learnt to understand one another's language. One day she complained to him that his father had beaten her with a stick several times as she went round and round tied to the yoke of the water-wheel. That day he experienced a feeling of hatred for his father, and refused to eat with him. His father tried to force him to eat by beating him with the same stick, but he refused obstinately and went to bed without supper.

When his daughter Nefissa was still a small child she used to wonder at the way he would talk to the buffalo. 'A buffalo can talk and understand just as we do,' he said to her many a time. Nefissa herself had not yet learnt how to speak, but she too seemed to understand what he was saying to her, and she would assure him with a look of her big, black, knowing eyes. She nodded her head and laughed, and sometimes would even stretch out her small hand and try to play with his whiskers. He opened his mouth, closed his lips over her smooth little fingers, and pretended to bite. She gurgled with laughter whenever he did this, and quickly pulled her hand away. But one day he really bit her finger with his teeth, as though he was about to eat it up. She screamed with pain, and backed away from him in fright. And from then on she started to be afraid of him sometimes, especially when for one reason or another his face would suddenly turn dark and forbidding, and begin to look like that of the buffalo. The face of the buffalo could put fear in her heart also, just as did the face of Kafrawi. She often played with her and pulled her tail, but all of a sudden a change would come over her, very much like the change which came over her father's face. Then her features no longer looked calm and resigned, but dark and angry. Her big eyes would be filled with a look which was very frightening, and at any moment she was capable of lashing out with her hoof, or butting at her with the head. On one occasion she even bit her badly on the leg.

Kafrawi rubbed his forehead against the full udder of the buffalo, opened his parched lips, and took the black nipple into his mouth. He could feel the warm milk flowing down to his stomach. His lids became relaxed, and dropped softly over his eyes. But the milk continued to flow further down to the lower part of his belly, and the upper part of his thighs. He felt something fill up, become swollen and erect, like a strange organ which was not a part of his body. He pressed on it with the palm of his hand, trying to push it back, but it refused to yield. He watched it get out, breaking through the limits of his body and his will, like a part of him over which he had lost control. Slowly it crept over the soft udder, breathing in the smell of female, lapping up the familiar wetness, slid up into the inner warmth and was lost in a great stillness, like an eternity, like death. After a while it tried to slip out into the fresh air again where it could breathe more freely, but the hole closed itself closely about it, like strong fingers intent on choking it to death. It fought for its life, jerked with the mad spasm of an animal caught in a trap, erupted itself of all capacity to fight and collapsed, like tired eyelids on tired eyes surrendering to the deepest of sleeps.

But a few moments later he opened his eyes again to the sound of a terrifying voice screaming out. The voice was not that of anyone human, whether man or woman. Nor was it the voice of some animal being beaten. It was a strange and fearful shriek.

He had heard it once before, a very long time ago. At the time he was lying on his belly on a dusty floor, with his mother squatting beside him. She was passing white flour through a fine sieve, but her eyes were fastened on him in a big black stare which neither blinked nor shifted elsewhere. He could feel them move over his features like the caress of a soft hand. Suddenly he heard the scream. He did not recognize his mother's voice in the awful shriek which rent the air. But his eyes were drawn to her unawares. Scattered all around her and covering her hands, and her face and her hair was a fine powder now spread out in a crimson layer. Her eyes were still wide open, fastened to him with the same fixed stare, but somehow their look was no longer the same, no longer had the expression which he knew so well. These were the eyes of someone else. His mother must have gone out through the open door and would be back any moment. He turned his head towards the door. He glimpsed two narrow, slit-like eyes which he had never seen before. They fixed him with a frightening stare. He bent his head, closed his eyes and dozed off for a while. But he was not really asleep, for he felt two arms lift him up from the ground and carry him away. He thought of opening his eyes to take a look around but he was afraid of meeting the terrible stare of the slit-like eyes, so he left himself to be carried by the two big arms. His face was pushed up against a hard, board-like chest from which emanated a strange odour. His small bare feet dangled down in the air, and swayed from side to side in rhythm with the long camel-like strides of the unknown creature that had snatched him from the ground, and was carrying him far away.

The scream rent the air a second time. He jumped up from where he lay, and without thinking ran towards the spot from which he heard the scream. It seemed to come from the middle of the field of maize, and to have been followed by a slight movement of the stalks around it. But now everything looked as still and as calm as it always had been, and the silence weighed heavily on the earth like the burning red rays of the sun throttling the slightest movement of the air before it even had a chance to stir.

As he came nearer, the field of maize split open suddenly at the same place. In the gap he saw two narrow, slit-like eyes appear for an instant, only to disappear a moment later. They vanished immediately as though the earth had opened to let them through, then quickly pulled them back into its depths, before he had the time to register what he had seen.

He thought he was dreaming. He watched his bare feet with the dark, cracked skin covering their heels walk slowly towards the spot in the middle of the field. His body shivered with some ancient, dark fear buried inside him. He tried to stop his feet, and for a moment it seemed as though they had come to a halt, and were no longer advancing across the field. But he soon realized that they continued to go forward at a steady pace, neither fast nor slow as though driven by a quiet, almost instinctive resolve to discover the unknown hidden somewhere ahead.

He pushed the maize stalks aside with his arms, and saw the body lying on the ground. All around it was a red-stained layer of dust and the wide-open staring eyes brought back a distant image of his mother lying dead on the ground. He put his hands around the face and moved it closer up, so that he could see her better. But the head was shaven like that of a man and she wore a man's *galabeya* around her body. When he looked into her eyes, he felt they were not the eyes of his mother, nor of any human being he had seen in his life. The sight of these strange eyes made him step back in a movement of fright, but before he could cover his face with his hands, and block out the sight, he felt a pair of strong hands clamp down on his back. A babble of hoarse voices interspersed with ugly shouts resounded in his ears. He turned round, and the noise increased. The faces crowded around him, and their eyes were staring, but some time passed before he was able to recognize the narrow, slit-like eyes of the Chief of the Village Guard, Sheikh Zahran.

# VII

All things seemed to move at the same slow, heavy pace. The red disc of the sun climbed down from the sky slow, ponderous and suffocating as it moved closer and closer to the earth before letting itself drop below the edge. The dark, plodding lines of peasants with their donkeys, cows and buffalo advanced in slow exhaustion over the dusty road to spill like a sticky fluid into the lanes and alleys leading to the houses and stables plunged in a sombre twilight. From the open doorways emanated the mixed odour of fermented manure, human excreta, and dough ready for baking. Before night enveloped the earth in its thick cloak all movement had ceased on the bank of the river, and neither man nor animal could any longer be seen on it. But the five-toed imprints of human feet, the flat rounded hoofs of donkeys, cows and buffalo could still be followed over the dusty trail interrupted now and then by the warm, rounded, freshly smelling clods of dung.

The body lying prostrate on the river bank however was no longer warm. The river breeze thrust against it gently, flapping

over the thin, old, worn cloak, and lifting it off the cracked heels
of what had once been the man Elwau.

A strong gust of wind pushed the cloak aside and uncovered
the lower part of the body. Through his heavy sleep-laden lids,
Haj Ismail glimpsed a long, hairy leg rising upwards to a full
muscular thigh. He lifted his eyelids with an effort and awakened suddenly, as though a brick had dropped on his head, sat
up with a jerk, and looked round, his eyes searching in different
directions. When his right eye looked straight in front, his left
eye seemed to look behind him, and when his left eye looked to
the right, his right eye turned to the left. He had come into the
world from his mother's womb with a squint. It was as though
for him each thing was split into two, or as though one single
thing became two, for while one eye was viewing what he wished
to see, the other was always struggling to be free.

He stood up, walked towards the body, and tugged at the
edge of the cloak to cover the naked limb. His hand touched
the hairy skin, and the swollen muscles underneath. A shiver
went through his body. He retreated quickly to where he had
been lying propped up against the river bank with the Chief
of the Village Guard sleeping soundly by his side. He curled
up and tried to fall asleep again, but the hairy muscular thigh
kept coming and going before his eyes. While one of his eyes
stared fixedly at it in fright, the other fled beneath his lid to
hide. His mind went back to a time when he was only ten. His
cousin Youssef was older and stronger than him. He had arms
and legs covered in hair, and the muscles of his thighs looked
like a swelling under the skin. When he saw them the first time
he was seized with fright, and tried to run away, but his cousin
had locked the door and there was no escape. He dodged this way
and that, but Youssef caught him in an iron grip holding him by

the back of his neck, threw him to the ground face downwards and wrenched his *galabeya* up over his buttocks. He felt the powerful, heavy body press down on him, and his nose hit the ground so that he could hardly breathe. After a while Youssef got up, opened the door and walked away. He lay there all day without moving, and when his father called out to him from the shop, he closed his eyes and pretended to be asleep. He heard his father's footsteps approaching, and his angry voice calling out again and again. He opened his mouth to answer, but no sound came out of his lips. A moment later a heavy fist landed on his back. He jumped to his feet and meekly followed behind his father to the shop at the corner of the lane where a few old cracked shelves carried packets of tea, or spice, or tobacco, and some cakes of soap.

His father taught him how to count the piastres, put them in the drawer, and then lock it with the key. He also taught him how to weigh tobacco on the balance by putting a piece in one pan, and a small weight in the other, so that the thick iron needle remained steady in the middle, and did not sway to one side.

Before closing the shop in the evening he would seat him on a bench next to him and teach him to give injections and open the abscesses of the people who came.

After the small *Eid* his father went on a pilgrimage to the Hejaz but never came back. He left him the shop, and a small bag with a pair of pincers for extracting teeth, verses of the Koran made into amulets, needles for injection, a razor for circumcising, and a bottle of iodine which had long since dried up.

Lying on the river bank he felt a painful headache begin to throb at the back of his head. He pulled out a handkerchief from his pocket, and tied it tightly around his head, then closed his eyes and tried to fall asleep, but just at that moment he saw a form which looked like some ghost approach the body where it lay on the river bank. He nudged the Chief of the Village Guard on the shoulder with his fist and said in a low voice, 'Sheikh Zahran.'

The Chief of the Village Guard sprang to his feet and shouted out, 'Who goes there?'

But no one answered.

He looked around carefully through his narrow, slit-like eyes but could see nothing, then started to walk in a wide circle round the dead body, shooting glances in different directions across the maize fields, or along the river bank and down its sloping side. Having failed to see anything which could hold his attention he returned to where the village barber sat cross-legged, but his eyes continued to shoot glances here and there into the night.

'What was it, Haj Ismail?' he asked.

'I could swear I saw a man, Haj Zahran.'

'Come on now! Go to sleep and leave matters in the hands of the Almighty God.'

'But I saw him come close to the body.'

'Who would think of stealing a body?'

'I tell you I saw him.'

'Could you recognize who it was?'

'No, I didn't see him well enough.'

'It must be the devil of Elwau hovering over him.'

'Devil? The only devils in this world are humans.'

He looked at the Chief of the Village Guard with one of his eyes and in a tone of feigned innocence asked, 'Was it a devil that killed Elwau?'

The Chief of the Village Guard answered quickly, 'No, it was Kafrawi.'

'Kafrawi is not capable of killing a chicken, and you know that very well,' said the village barber.

'But when it's a man's honour that's at stake, anyone can kill,' said the Chief of the Village Guard heatedly.

'You can tell that to the villagers, or to the officer who will conduct the inquest, but not to me,' said Haj Ismail. 'I see that this time you want to kill two birds with one stone. But speaking seriously, who is the killer this time?'

The Chief of the Village Guard gave a sharp laugh and then yawningly said, 'Allah alone knows.'

Haj Ismail looked at him again with one eye. 'You know them all without exception, and can name any one of them.'

This time it was the turn of Sheikh Zahran to put on an innocent air. 'Now who can you be referring to, Haj Ismail?' he said.

The village barber chuckled in a knowing way. 'Whoever it is, the officer will be coming in the morning with the police dogs.'

'Do you think dogs know better than human beings?' asked the Chief of the Village Guard sarcastically. 'Everyone says that Kafrawi killed Elwau because of Nefissa. As a matter of fact, quite a number of people saw him kneeling next to his body with blood on his hands. He is steeped in this crime from the top of his head to the bottom of his heels.'

The village barber chuckled again. 'You are really the son of a devil, Sheikh Zahran.'

'I am the obedient servant of him who gives us our orders.' He yawned indifferently. 'In fact, all of us are his obedient servants.'

'All of us serve God.'

'What matters is that we are all servants. No matter how high we rise, or how low we fall, the truth is that we are all slaves, serving someone.'

'We are God's slaves when it's time to say our prayers only. But we are the Mayor's slaves all the time.'

Sheikh Zahran's eyes shone as he whispered in the ear of the village barber.

'Do you know that he does not sleep the night because of Zeinab? I have done my best to convince her but she still refuses.'

'Kafrawi must be encouraging her to refuse. Do you think he has started to become suspicious?' queried the village barber.

The Chief of the Village Guard hastened to refute this possibility.

'No, absolutely not. Suspicion requires that a man be endowed with a brain that can think. But these peasants! They have no brain, and when they do have one, it's like the brain of a buffalo. The problem is that after Nefissa left, Kafrawi has no one to help in the house, or work in the fields except Zeinab. I've been telling him all the time that the Mayor will give him ten whole pounds for her work, that she will eat and drink in his house, and live in the kind of comfort she could never ever dream of. All she will have to do is sweep and clean the house, and she can go home at the end of the day's work. But he won't listen to me. His head is harder than stone.'

'His daughter Zeinab is just as pig-headed as he is. I've done all I can to convince her, explained everything to her in detail, but she's like a mule,' said Haj Ismail. 'I can't see any advantages to her. There's not a girl in Kafr El Teen who has not got more manners and more beauty than she has.'

Sheikh Zahran lowered his voice. 'He's got strange tastes where women are concerned, and if he likes a woman he can't forget her. You know he's pretty obstinate himself. Once he sets his eyes on a woman he must have her, come what may.'

Haj Ismail opened his mouth in a big, prolonged yawn. 'Why not? People like him who live on top of the world, don't know the word impossible.'

'They walk over the earth like Gods.'

'No, Sheikh Zahran, they're Gods all right but they don't walk, they ride in cars. Walking is for people like us.'

'Walking only? You seem to forget that we also sleep on the ground.'

The Chief of the Village Guard curled himself up under his cloak and closed his eyes. Haj Ismail threw a last quick look at the body lying on the river bank before curling up under his cloak in turn. He murmured in a low voice, 'What a shame. Elwau was really too young to die.'

The Chief of the Village Guard heard him and sighed. 'Our lives are in God's hands, Haj Ismail.'

'Yes verily, that's true. It's Allah alone who decides when it's time for us to leave this earth.'

And so they went to sleep with the firm knowledge that the life of people in Kafr El Teen depended on one God ever-present in their minds. They spent many an evening talking to him in front of the village barber's shop, or on the terrace of his house overlooking the Nile. They knew that he burned with such a desire for Zeinab that only death could put an end to it. Sooner or later he was going to lay his hands on her, for like all Gods he believed that the impossible did not exist.

The noise of their snoring rose into the night from under the bank of the river where they had sought shelter. It travelled through the silent night to reach the ears of Metwalli as he lay hidden between the stalks of maize. He emerged out of the field and went straight towards the body. He advanced with wary steps, leaning on his right leg more heavily than he did on the left.

He had a characteristic way of walking, well-known by the inhabitants of Kafr El Teen, very much like a limping dog. An old childhood affliction of the bones had left him with one leg shorter than the other.

He emerged over the top of the river bank. The light of the moon shone down on him revealing a head which looked big compared with the body. His small eyes were buried in a swollen face, and his thick lips protruded under a thin nose. His lower lip hung down towards his chin, revealing its inner smooth belly, and his saliva drooled continuously over it on to the long beard.

If the children of the village had spotted him at this moment, they would have followed behind him shouting out in unison, 'Here goes the idiot.' One of them might even have thrown a stone at him, or pulled him by the edge of his *galabeya*. But he would have continued to walk, paying no attention to them, with the saliva streaming down from his mouth on to his chest, as he moved on, panting and limping like a stray dog. People would meet him moving through the lanes, his wet eyes gazing at the houses and the passers-by with a dull, unseeing look, his thick lips open and drooling the spit of his mouth as he went along. At the end of each day he could be seen sitting near the cemetery at the far end of the river bank, scratching his head and his body, or holding the lice between his fingers before he cracked them under his nails.

If one of the village women passed him by, she would throw him half a loaf of bread, or a corn cob, or a mulberry fruit, aiming it at his open lap. Sometimes she would touch him and say, 'Give me your blessings, Sheikh Metwalli.' Then he would stop scratching, or cracking his lice for a moment, stretch out his hand to her, and take hold of whatever part of her body his fingers happened to touch whether it be her shoulder, her hand, her leg, or any other part, squeeze it, and mutter a few unintelligible words as the white flow of saliva meandered down over his black beard.

It was said that a woman afflicted with paralysis had touched him and been cured, and that he had helped a blind man to regain his sight. He had been chosen by God, knew about sickness, and could penetrate the secrets of the future. Allah had bestowed his powers on him since Allah chose the weakest of all His creatures for His purposes. And so they called him Sheikh Metwalli.

But Haj Ismail, the village barber, chose to describe him as 'the possessed one'; Sheikh Zahran, the Chief of the Village Guard, named him 'the lousy one'; and the children addressed him as 'Metwalli the idiot.' As far as he was concerned, he was Metwalli, the son of Sheikh Osman, who used to recite verses of the Koran over the souls of the deceased buried in the cemetery. But Sheikh Osman was now dead, and all he had bequeathed him was his torn caftan, his turban, a bread basket empty of bread, and an old Koran with half its cover torn off.

Now he was advancing with much less of a limp than he put on when people were around. His eyes had a steady gaze which no one had seen in them before, and every now and then he turned round cautiously. His lower lip no longer hung down over his chin, and the saliva had ceased to flow out of his mouth. Any of the inhabitants of the village seeing him at this moment would not have recognized him.

He was moving towards the body where it lay on the river bank, covered with a cloak. Within a short distance of it, he dropped on his belly and started to crawl over the ground. Reaching the feet, he lifted the cloak, poked his head in underneath, and drew his body slowly up over the legs and thighs.

If the Chief of the Village Guard had happened to open his eyes at that moment, he would not have noticed any change. The cloak still covered the body in the same way. There might have been a very slight movement which rose and fell like some imperceptible wave, but it seemed to be more like a movement of the air than of anything else. Besides no other possibility would have occurred to the Chief of the Village Guard, nor to any man or woman of blood and flesh, or even to one of the devilish spirits that roam around in many places, especially those chosen by the living for the dead. For after all, what was lying on the river bank was no more than a body from which all life had fled, and who apart from the worms which burrow into everything could be interested in the dead?

But Metwalli had lived among the dead year after year, like any worm. Every day he would squat in his usual place at the far end of the village, on the river bank, waiting until the sun had dropped into some deep recess. Then he stood up, descended the slope of the river bank with his limping gait, and walked slowly in the direction of the cemetery to seek his bed among the dead. But once arrived there, before lying down to rest, he wandered between the rows of graves, bending down every now and then to pick up a piece of pastry or bread left by some relative of one of the dead. Even after he had eaten, he remained awake for some time, as though turning something over in his mind before he slept. Then suddenly he stood up again, and walked straight to one of the graves, guided in the dark by a certain smell which he knew so well that he could distinguish it even at a distance, and even if surrounded by other smells. It was the smell of new buried flesh, of warm blood and cells which still lived although the body was dead.

He dug the ground feverishly with his strong wiry fingers, as sharp and as cutting as those of a cat, searching for a piece of meat buried in the ground. With hands trained by this oft-repeated exercise he tore away the shroud of white cloth, rolled it up tightly into a spherical mass, and buried it in a hole dug in the ground. He covered it with earth and left it until he would return to dig it up in the early hours of the next morning while people still slept.

Once over with this task, he turned his attention to the still warm body of the dead. If it was that of a female, he would crawl over it until his face was near the chin. But if the body was male, he turned it over on its face, then crawled over it until the lower part of his belly pressed down on the buttocks from behind.

In the morning Metwalli would disappear from Kafr El Teen. No one troubled to look for him, or to wonder where he could be. But some distance away at Ramla or Bauhout he sat on the pavement of a crowded street, right in the middle of the weekly market bargaining over the sale of some yards of dusty white sheeting which no one knew had served a few hours earlier as a shroud for some dead body buried quite recently in the cemetery of Kafr El Teen.

# VIII

The car entered the village preceded by its high-pitched horn, and followed by a storm of dust, a swarm of children and some stray dogs. Out of it stepped some gentlemen, one of whom was followed by a male nurse carrying a bag, and the second by a policeman holding back a dog which kept tugging at its leash. A group of men were busy walking up and down trying to push the people standing around as far back as they could, or lashing out at the buttocks of the children with their canes.

The whole village of Kafr El Teen had gathered on the bank of the river. The men wore *galabeyas* and each held a stick. The women had wrapped themselves in black shawls. The children were surrounded by clouds of flies, and exhibited bare buttocks and running noses. Everyone was there. Only three people were missing. Zakeya sat squatting as usual in the dusty entrance to her house, with Zeinab beside her. Both were silent, their angry, almost defiant eyes gazing into the lane.

Kafrawi also sat squatting but much further away on the outskirts of the village trying to hide between the maize stalks in a field. From his hiding place he could hear voices coming closer, preceded by the yapping, barking and whining of the dog. He realized that they must have found out where he was hiding, so he stepped out of the maize field and clambered up the bank of the river. Some of the children spotted him and cried out, 'Kafrawi, Kafrawi!', then started to run after him but he ran faster and arrived at the edge of the river. Before the dog tugging furiously at its leash with the policeman running behind it, had time to pounce on him he had thrown himself into the water. He did not know why he was running away, or where he was going.

He was just putting as much distance as he could between himself and something he feared, just going without knowing where to go. He did not know what had happened to him since the moment when he had been lying with the buffalo, until the moment when his body struck cold water.

He heard a splashing in the water and realized that someone was swimming rapidly towards him, getting closer and closer. He lunged out with his arms and legs, straining his sight to see the other shore as though there he would find safety and security. He had forgotten that on the other shore were the orange orchards owned by the Mayor of Kafr El Teen.

On the river bank were gathered the inhabitants of Kafr El Teen. They stood slightly in the background, and in front of them was a group composed of the officer with his dog, the Chief of the Village Guard, some of the village guards, and a few district policemen. Their eyes followed the two bodies swimming in the river, with the zeal of spectators watching a race, and wondering who of the two would be the winner. When the distance between the two swimmers increased the villagers would experience a secret feeling of joy, for they were hoping that Kafrawi would manage to escape, and that the policeman would fail to catch up with him. Instinctively they felt Kafrawi was not a killer, or a criminal. They hated the policeman and his dogs, hated all policemen, all officers, all representatives of authority and the government. It was the hidden ancient hatred of peasants for their government. They knew that in some way or another they had always been the victims, always been exploited, even if most of the time they could not understand how it was happening.

The officer was watching the scene with a cold detachment, looking at his wrist watch every now and then as though he had an important appointment, and wanted to be over with this mission as quickly as possible. The dog also did not seem to care much about what was happening. It was lying on the river bank enjoying the sunshine, the green fields and the expanses of water as though long deprived of a chance to enjoy such natural beauty. The only person who seemed nervous was the Chief of the Village Guard. Every time the distance between the two swimmers decreased, he would shout out encouragingly, 'Well done, Bayumi!'

His voice echoed in the ears of Bayumi like a clarion call, making him lunge out with his arms and legs more vigorously. Why this was so he could not himself understand. He had been assigned the task of capturing this animal, and that was all. Further than that his mind refused to go. From the moment when the order 'Arrest him' had resounded in his ears, he had launched himself in pursuit of the man like a projectile fired from a gun.

Kafrawi's naked body stepped out of the water and leapt on to the shore threading its way through the trees of the orchard. Bayumi followed close behind, his body also naked except for the pair of baggy singlets which he still wore. He was tall, with wiry muscles, and his face, too, looked hard and narrow with sharp features which remained as rigid as cardboard. It was the face of a policeman expressing neither joy nor sadness, fear nor hope, a face without feeling carrying an expressionless expression which says nothing at all. A face without features like the palm of a hand from which you can glean no feeling or thought, because they have been suppressed for so long that nothing is left any more, or a face made of bronze, or copper like the knocker which hangs on doors, and is used to alert people in the house that there is someone outside who wants to intrude just when they feel most cosy and warm. His body too was hard and copper-like, with arms and legs which ran or swam or walked with a steady, swinging, untiring movement, so unchanging, so enduring that it could hardly be human, hardly come from a body of flesh and blood and bone, but only from a robot with metal limbs and joints.

Kafrawi saw him as he hid behind a tree. His body shook with a strange fear as though he had seen something which was neither man nor devil, neither live nor dead, some evil spirit which was not human despite its human form.

He felt this fear sweep over him like a wave of icy cold water. He could no longer follow his body, understand what it was doing, know whether it was hiding behind the orange trees or threading its way between them. For tracking him down was the frightening shadow, moving at a machine-like pace neither fast nor slow, like the hands of a clock moving steadily towards the hour of execution, so that when the steely fingers closed around his arm he felt his time had come and quietly whispered, 'Verily I do witness that there is no other God than Allah.' Then everything went black and he could no longer hear or see anything. The dark was so stock still that it seemed as though his life had come to a sudden end, and now was the moment ordained for him to go.

When he came to again, and began to hear and see once more, his eyes looked around him in great astonishment. He was squatting in a huge room crowded with people, and they kept throwing glances towards him. In front of him were three men sitting behind something high which looked like a table.

One of the three men was gesturing with his hand angrily, and fixing him with his eyes, in a menacing way. He looked around again trying to understand what was happening. Suddenly he felt a pointed finger jab into his shoulder like a nail, and a thin sharp voice pierced his ear. 'Have you not heard? Why don't you answer?'

Kafrawi opened his mouth and asked, 'Is someone speaking to me?'

The thin, sharp voice cut through the air again. 'Yes, are you asleep? Wake up, and answer His Excellency's questions.'

Kafrawi could not figure out who His Excellency could be, nor could he understand where he now was. He was certainly no longer in Kafr El Teen. He could be in another village, or even in another world. He wondered how they had carried him to this place, and how he had got here.

Suddenly he heard an angry voice say to him, 'What's your name?'

He answered, 'Kafrawi.'

The angry voice came back at him. 'Your age?'

He hesitated for a moment before saying, 'Forty or fifty.'

He heard people laugh and could not understand why they did so.

The angry voice resumed. 'You are accused of having murdered Elwau and it's better for you to admit to your crime, instead of beating about the bush.'

'Admit to what?' he asked.

'Admit to killing Elwau.'

'I did not kill him. Elwau was a good man.'

The voice said, 'Did you not hear that he was the man who assaulted your daughter, Nefissa?'

' I heard them say it was Elwau.'

'After you heard that, did you not think of killing him?'

'No.'

The voice asked, 'Why?'

'I did not think of it.'

'Is that normal for a man whose honour has been sullied?'

'I don't know,' Kafrawi answered.

The voice sounded very angry. 'Is that natural?'

'What does natural mean?'

He heard laughter again. He looked around in surprise. He could not understand why people kept laughing. It occurred to him that they might be laughing about something which had nothing to do with him.

The voice resumed its questioning. 'On that Friday, why did you stay in the fields instead of going to the mosque for prayer like all the men of the village?'

'I've stopped praying since Nefissa left.'

'Why?'

'Nefissa used to look after the buffalo while I went to pray.'

'Did you not know that, unlike the other men in the village, Elwau did not go to the mosque on Fridays?'

'Yes.'

'Did you or did you not know?'

'I knew. Everybody knew that Elwau did not go to the mosque.'

'Why?'

'I don't know why. People say that his mother's grandfather was a Copt, but Allah alone knows the reason.'

The voice asked insinuatingly, 'Did you dislike Elwau?'

'No.'

'Was it not your conviction that a man like him should have carried out the religious rites which Allah has ordained?'

Kafrawi said, 'Elwau was a good man.'

'Do you not know that prayer is a protection against sin?'

'Yes, that's what Sheikh Hamzawi used to say to us.'

'So Elwau assaulted your daughter and committed a grievous sin.'

'That's what was said.'

'And after all that happened, you insist you didn't think of killing him?'

'No, I didn't.'

'Why did you not think of killing him?'

'Elwau was a good man,' Kafrawi repeated.

The voice came back, insistent. 'Don't you care about honour? Don't you care about your honour and that of your family?'

Kafrawi was silent for a moment and then replied, 'Yes, I do.'

The voice said with a note of triumph barely veiled, 'That's why you killed Elwau.'

'But I did not kill him.'

The voice was very angry again. 'Then why were you found near the body?'

Kafrawi was silent, trying to remember, but his memory failed him. He said nothing.

The voice still sounded angry. 'Why did you run away and try to escape?'

'I was afraid of the dog.'

'Do you know why the dog picked you out from all the men in the village?'

'No. It's the dog who knows.'

He heard laughter in the room and looked around in great surprise. Why were people laughing again?

The voice was furious this time. 'Don't try to deceive me. You had better confess. Do you know what's awaiting you?'

'No,' he said.

Laughter echoed in his ears once more. His eyes expressed a puzzled amazement. After a moment he felt the steely fingers close round his arm as they led him away into a long, dark passage. He closed his eyes and muttered, 'I do testify that there is no God but Allah.'

# IX

Zakeya still sat on the dusty threshold with Zeinab by her side. Both of them were plunged in silence, and their eyes continued to watch the lane with an expression of angry defiance. In front of them there still rose the huge door with its iron bars. It seemed to stand there blocking the way, shutting out the bank of the river and the water which flowed beside it. From time to time the Mayor walked out, tall, broad-shouldered, surrounded by men on all sides. He walked ahead of them with his slow steady stride. In his eyes was the haughty, blue look which he raised to the skies. He never bent his head to look at the ground over which he walked, nor noticed Zakeya and Zeinab sitting on the dusty threshold of their house, thinking over something in silence, their eyes staring in front of them steadily.

Zakeya's hands rested on her lap, over her wide, black *galabeya*. They were big, and the skin on them was coarse and cracked. In her palm lay the deep imprint of the hoe which she held firmly in her clasp whenever she dug into the soil. Her nails were black, and they smelt of manure and of mud. Now and again she would lift them from her lap to hold her head, or wipe the sticky sweat, or chase away a mosquito or a gnat. Zeinab sat by her side, her hands busy sifting the corn from the chaff, or kneading the dung with straw, and cutting it into round cakes like a loaf of bread. Sometimes she would stand up, lift the earthenware jar to her head and walk to the river bank. Her body was tall and slender, her big, dark eyes faced straight ahead. She did not look at passers-by, or houses on the way, or shops or sheds. Nor did she smile at anyone, or greet a friend as the other girls or women did. When she passed in front of Haj Ismail's shop she would hasten her pace. She could almost feel the blue eyes singe her back. They gazed at her fixedly, inflexibly, cruelly cutting through her dress, feeding on the beauty of her legs, on the curving flesh, on the fullness of her thighs and belly, on the petal-like skin and the waist narrow and slender above her hips, on her back rising up like a powerful stem.

She would lift her shawl to hide her face and cover her breast. But the sharp, inflexible eyes which knew no rest, no quiet, no tenderness, pierced through her robe as she climbed the river bank, or descended its sloping flank, slid over her back, and round her uncovered body to the pointed breasts which moved up and down with every step, with the beat of her heart and the rhythm of her breath. She advanced quickly, her eyes fixed straight ahead, cheeks flushed with health, full lips trembling, her lithe form wafted through the open spaces as though on air.

When she got home she would lift the earthenware jar of water from her head, and put it on the ground, then sit down by the side of her Aunt Zakeya still out of breath. Her heart continued to beat fast under her ribs, her chest heaved up and down, and the drops of sweat stood out on her forehead, for they had not yet dried, nor had they dripped down over her face to disappear over her neck.

Zakeya would stare at her silently for some time. Then her parched lips would part and in a low, tense whisper she would ask, 'What's wrong with you, my child?'

But Zeinab never answered, so Zakeya would drop into silence again for a long while before her lips opened again with the oft repeated lament.

'I wonder where you are, Galal my son. I wonder whether you are alive or dead. O God, if I knew he was dead my mind would be put at rest. And now Kafrawi has also been taken away. Who knows if he'll ever come back. O God, were not Galal and Nefissa enough? Did you have to take Kafrawi also? We no longer have anyone left, and the house is empty. Zeinab is still young and I am old. Who is going to look after the buffalo and the crops?'

Zeinab dried her sweat on her shawl and then she said, 'I have grown up now, and I will look after the buffalo, and the crops, and the house and everything else until my father comes back. Father will come back, and so will Galal, and Nefissa as well.'

'Those that go never come back, my child.'

'God knows what difficult straits we're in and He won't abandon us.'

Zakeya muttered in a low tone as though speaking to herself. 'No one is going to come back. Those who go never come back. Kafrawi too. He will not return.'

'My father will come back. You will see. He'll come back,' Zeinab said vehemently. 'He will tell them that he did not kill anyone and they will believe him. Everybody knows my father is a kind man, and could never kill anybody.'

The old woman sighed. 'People here know him. But over there, no one knows who he is. If Galal was here he would have gone with him. Galal knows the people there, and he could have helped him. But Galal is not here. He used to lend a helping hand to everyone, even to strangers, so you can imagine what it would have been like with his uncle Kafrawi.'

'May Allah come to his aid.'

'My child, Allah alone is not enough.'

Zeinab opened her big black eyes wide, and looked at her with amazement. 'God Almighty have mercy on us. God is great and helps everyone. Aunt, why don't you get up, do your ablutions, and pray God to help us.'

Zakeya raised her hands in a gesture of rebuttal. 'I have not ceased praying and begging God to help us. And yet every day our misery becomes greater, and we are afflicted with a new suffering.'

Her voice was not angry. It was distant, and calm, and as cold as ice. Zeinab's eyes opened even wider with astonishment. She was gazing up at the heavens with a strange expression in her eyes. Zeinab was seized with a dark shiver that made the hair on her body stand up. Her hands were shaking as she took hold of Zakeya's hand and held it between them.

'What's the matter, Aunt?' she asked anxiously. 'Your hand is as cold as ice.'

Zakeya did not answer. She continued to stare into space with her wide open black eyes. Zeinab's hand was still shaking as she held her shoulder and pressed it.

'What's the matter, Aunt? Please tell me what's the matter with you,' she implored.

But Zakeya still continued to stare in front of her in silence like a statue. The girl was seized with terror. She clapped her hands to her face in agony and screamed, 'My Aunt Zakeya. O God, something has happened to my Aunt Zakeya.'

Almost immediately the yard of the house was filled with the dark forms of people. They crowded through the dusty entrance of the house, and filled up the yard and the lane outside, coming between Zakeya and the huge iron gate on which she had fixed her eyes. But she could still see the big iron bars moving towards her as she lay on her belly over the ground. They came closer and closer like long iron legs which would crush her at any moment. She licked the dust with her tongue, and a sticky wetness streamed from her mouth, her nose and her eyes on to the ground. She screamed as loudly as she could to make sure that her mother would hear her, and snatch her up quickly from under the long legs of the buffalo that looked as though they would walk over her at any moment. And her mother arrived just in the nick of time to save her from being crushed. It was a strange dream which had visited her many times in her sleep. Other nights she would dream that she was standing on a hill. Suddenly her body fell from on high into the river and started to drown. But she swam with all her might, although she did not know how, and managed to reach the river bank. She was about to lift herself out of the water on to the ground when she found herself in front of a huge iron gate. She was lying on a mat with her husband Abdel Moneim on one side and her son Galal on the other. She opened her eyes to the sound of their breathing. From behind the iron bars of a window she could see a man pushing a hand cart filled up with calves' feet and heads, and entrails. Blood kept dripping from the cart on to the dust. The stranger's eyes were fixed on her as he came nearer. His long arm stretched out and tried to pull off the anklet she wore around her leg. When he was close enough she could see that his eyes were those of Om Saber who now leant over her and tried to push one thigh away from the other. Then she pulled out a razor

blade from somewhere and proceeded to cut her neck. She tried
to scream, but her voice would not come out. Then she tried to
run, but her feet were nailed to the ground. When she turned
her head, she could see her son Galal sleeping beside her. She
tried to put her arm around him but he seemed to move out of
reach, and suddenly a hand caught hold of her on the other side.
She looked round to find her husband fast asleep, but he got up
at once, and started to hit her on her head, and chest. Then he
kicked her in her belly which was pregnant with child. She tried
to scream again, but her voice did not come out and when she
looked at him he had come very close and was busy tearing her
*galabeya* down the front till her body was exposed. She could
feel his fingers around her breast, feel them creep down to her
belly and between her thighs. His heavy body bore down upon
her with all its strength, pressing harder and harder down on
her flesh, so that the ground beneath her began to shake. When
she opened her eyes again the face of her husband Abdel Moneim
had disappeared and in its place, right in front of her was the
face of her brother Kafrawi. She screamed out as loudly as she
could but no one seemed to hear her voice. Kafrawi hid his face
in the mat and wept bitterly. She stretched out her hand to him
and lifted his head, but when she looked at his face, it was the
face of her son Galal. She wiped the tears in his eyes with the
palm of her hand, then washed his nose and mouth with water
from the earthenware jar held up by the iron stand in the corner
of the room. Around him formed a pool of water and liquid stools
but after a short while the ground had started to become dry, but
the dryness crept up to her son's body. It shrank rapidly before
her eyes, and became the size of a small rabbit, so she dug a hole
and buried him in the ground. Just at that moment her husband
came back from the fields, and because he could not find his son

anywhere he started to beat her again. For it was like that. Every time a son of hers died he would strike out at her blindly, and beat her up with anything he could lay his hands on. And the same thing would happen whenever she gave birth to a daughter. She had given birth to ten sons and six daughters – but the only child who had lived to grow up was Galal. All the others had died at different ages, for life was like that. One never knew when a child would die.

She looked around at the circle of staring eyes, and said in a low voice, 'Galal is the only one that grew up to live. But now he has gone and will not return. Kafrawi also is gone, and Nefissa. The house is empty, and Zeinab is young. And I am too old to be of much use. There is no longer anyone to look after the buffalo, and tend to the crops.'

She heard a chorus of voices say in one breath, 'God is great, Zakeya. Pray to Him that He send them back to you safely,' and without looking at them she replied, 'Many a time have I prayed to God, called upon Him, beseeched Him to have mercy on us, but He never seemed to hear me, or to respond.'

And the voices cried out as though with one voice, 'Have mercy on her for what she has said, O God. Have mercy on us. Thou alone art all-powerful. Without Thee we are helpless, and without strength.'

# X

Zakeya still squatted on the ground, in the same place. She would close her eyes, then open them, then close them again. If she closed her eyes she could see the huge door, or the window with its iron bars, and the man behind it pushing a cartful of calves' feet and heads, and entrails dripping with blood. He tried to pull her by the foot, then by the leg and slaughter her with a big knife. She would open her eyes in terror, and look at the faces gathered around her. The only faces she could recognize were those of her niece Zeinab, and Om Saber, as she sat cross-legged on the ground in front of a tin pot placed over the kerosene stove. White clouds of steam smelling of incense rose up in the air, mingling with the babble of voices and of words she could not make out. She could see the gestures, and the movements of the men and women gathered around, but could not figure out what they were doing there. A group of women were circling around the steaming pot as though dancing. Their breasts and their buttocks shook up and down to the powerful beat of a drum, and the long tresses of their loose hair whirled round and round. Their mouths gaped open as they repeated the slow chant: 'O thou Sheikh whom the spirits obey, let him who carries the evil spirit within him be rid of it at once.' A group of men were shaking and shivering to the beat of the drums. They wore white turbans with a long tail that hung down behind their backs.

Om Saber kept coming and going between the crowd of men and women, her body draped in a long *melaya*. Her body was short and skinny with flat breasts, but her buttocks were big and shook violently as she whirled amidst the throngs of dancing people. From the front she looked like a man, but seen from the back she looked like a woman. Her quick, energetic movements gave an impression of youth, but her face was wizened and old. When dancing with the men she moved her body and slapped them on the hips in exactly the same way as she did with the women. She danced and laughed, then the next moment slapped her face with her hands and shrieked in agony. When she told dirty stories it was with the same voice as she recited verses of the Koran, or incantations. No one thought badly of what she did. For the villagers of Kafr El Teen she was Om Saber, the *daya*, neither man nor woman, but an asexual being without a family, or relatives or offspring. She lived in a dark mud hut adjoining the hut of Nafoussa the dancer. It was located behind a piece of waste land, near the mosque. No one knew when she had arrived in the village, where she came from, or when she had been born. People did not even imagine she would die, for they always saw her on the move from morning till night, going from house to house, helping the women in labour, circumcising the girls or piercing holes in their ears, sprinkling salt in the house the week after a child had been born, consoling wives on the fortieth day after their husbands had died, in fact participating in every occasion for festivity or mourning. At weddings she would lead the *yoo yoos*, paint the feet of girls and women with red henna, and on the wedding night she would tear the virgin's hymen with her finger, or conceal the fact that it was already torn by spraying the white towel on which the virgin's blood was supposed to pour with the blood of a rabbit or a hen. But when it was a time for mourning her suffering knew no bounds. She would slap her face with both hands repeatedly, scream out in agony, chant a hymn of sadness to the deceased, and wash the body if she was a female. She was always busy solving the problems of girls and women, carrying out abortions with a stalk of *mouloukheya*, throttling the new-born baby if necessary, or leaving it to die by not tying the umbilical cord with a silk thread so that it bled to death.

All the inhabitants of Kafr El Teen knew her well. She was a part of every household, and no household could survive without her. She brought couples together in lawful matrimony, arranged marriages, found suitable husbands for the girls, and prospective brides for the men, protected the good name of families and the chastity of young females, and helped to conceal whatever could sully their honour, or cause a scandal, or result in a catastrophe, or be looked upon as a sign of disloyalty between husbands and wives. She treated sick people with popular remedies, participated in the rites of *zar*, danced and sang, slaughtered animals and sprayed their blood, burnt incense, and discovered the hiding places in which people had concealed things. And when it so happened that she was not engaged in any of these activities, she would carry a huge basket on her head and go around the houses selling handkerchiefs, incense, chewing gum and snuff, or telling fortunes, and reading the future in people's cups.

The sweat was pouring out of Zakeya's face as she lay pros-trate on the ground, or when she squatted or stood up. She moved from one position to the other in a kind of stupor so that she could not tell in which position she was at a particular moment. All around bodies shivered, and shook, and swayed, falling to the ground and standing up again. Sweat welled out from every pore of their skin. She could tell the women from the way their breasts and their buttocks were shaking, and the men from the movement of the dark whiskers and long beards around their faces.

The sweat continued to pour out of her body in an endless stream. She kept lifting her hand to wipe it away from her brow and face, but each time her hand came away stained a deep red. For Om Saber repeatedly filled her cupped hands with the blood of a cock which she had slaughtered herself, and sprayed it over Zakeya's face and body. One of the men dipped his hand into the blood and took turns at spraying her with it. She felt his hand slip through the neck of her *galabeya*, and cover her breasts with wet sticky blood. After this many hands crowded in on her body, touching or pinching or squeezing parts of it and spraying more blood until she was soaking in it all over. At one moment a heavy hand moved up between her legs and covered the parts between the thighs with blood. She could not tell whether it was the hand of a woman or a man, but it pinched her roughly. She clapped her hands over her face and emitted a series of shrieks as though she had lost control of herself. She could hear the people around her chanting madly, 'O thou Sheikh whom the spirits obey, let him who bears the evil spirit within him come out with it at once.' The screaming and wailing was mingled in her ears with the beating of drums, and the stamping of feet. Everything seemed to merge into one, sweat and blood, man and woman, features of one face with features of the other, so that nothing was any longer distinguishable. She could no longer tell Om Saber's features from those of Sheikh Metwalli or the difference between Zeinab and Nafoussa the dancer. Zeinab's body seemed to have become taller, its curves were more pronounced, and it swayed and reeled like the body of Nafoussa the dancer. Her hair was undone, and its tresses swung freely in the air in exactly the same way as Nafoussa's hair had gone wild around her head. It looked longer than it had ever looked before, and jutted out in every direction. She tossed it in front of her with a sudden bending of the head, so that it covered her pointed breasts, then threw it back with an upswing of her head, and let its lower ends leap over the moving curves of her hips. Her *galabeya* had split from its tail up to her waist, and when she stamped with her foot it swung open revealing the smooth skin of her thighs and legs. Every time she struck the ground with her foot, the material rent, and the split crept higher up. Now through the opening one could see her breast, the lines of her belly, the frenzy of her dancing flesh. The bodies around her swayed, and reeled, and fell, only to stand up again. The men and the women now joined in one circle which went round and round. In the middle of the circle danced Nafoussa and Sheikh Metwalli. Each time he moved his hand, or his knee, or his foot he would touch her thigh, or her belly, or her breast. She would catch hold of her long hair, pull it with all her strength, and scream at the top of her voice, 'O thou Sheikh whom the spirits obey, let him who carries the evil spirit be rid of it at once.' Sheikh Metwalli and everyone else would join in the same chant, screaming as wildly and as loudly as they could.

It seemed to Zakeya as though her body was now moving of its own accord, or obeying a will of its own. She saw her feet walk towards the circle of people who were dancing. Her body pushed its way through among the other bodies, and started to move with them, to shake and reel in the same way. The woollen thread with which she tied her hair slipped off, and her hair floated down over her face like some black cloud. She felt a hand touch her breast, and the strong fingers sink into the flesh with a pain that was more sharp than the bite of a snake. She opened her mouth wide and started to scream and to wail in a continuous high-pitched lament, as though mourning the suffering of a whole lifetime suppressed in her body from the very first moment of her life when her father struck her mother on the head because she had not borne him the son he expected. It was a wail that went back, far back, to many a moment of pain in her life. To the times when she ran behind the donkey and the hot earth burnt the soles of her feet. To the times when she learnt to eat the salted pickles and green peppers which the peasants consume with their bread, and felt something like a slow fire deep down inside the walls of her belly. To the time when Om Saber forced her thighs apart and with her razor cut off a piece of her flesh. To the time when she developed two breasts which the menfolk would pinch when there was nobody around to prevent them. To the time when her spouse Abdel Moneim would beat her with his stick, then climb on her and bear down on her chest with all his weight. To the time when she bore him children and bled, then buried them one after the other with the dead. To the time when Galal put on his army uniform and never came back, and the time when Nefissa ran away, and the children's chorus rang out as they sang 'Nefissa and Elwau.' To the time when the car came to the village carrying the gentlemen from town and the dog, then took Kafrawi with them and left.

Her wail went back and back to such times and others she could not forget like a lament which has no end, and sees no end to all the pain in life. It seemed to be as long as the length of her life, as long as the long hours of her days and nights. It went on and on as she tugged at her hair with all her might, tore her garment to shreds, and dug her nails into the flesh of her body as though she wanted to tear herself apart. It went on and on as Om Saber continued to fill her cupped hands with the blood of the slaughtered cock, and spray it over her face, and her neck, and over her body at the front and the back.

'Scream, Zakeya!' she cried out. 'Chase the evil spirit out of your body. Scream as loud and as long as you can.'

Now they were all screaming at the top of their voices. Zakeya and Om Saber, Nafoussa and Zeinab, Sheikh Metwalli and all the men and women of Kafr El Teen who were gathered around. Their voices joined in a high-pitched wail, as long as the length of their lives, reaching back to those moments in time when they had been born, and beaten and bitten and burnt under the soles of their feet, and in the walls of their stomach, since the bitterness flowed with their bile, and death snatched their sons and their daughters, one after the other in a line.

# XI

But the devil refused to leave Zakeya's body. It continued to dwell within her, to ride on her back, and jump on her chest. She gasped as though out of breath when she sat up, watched him snuggle up against her chest and look at her with the eyes of Galal. She would pull out her breast from the neck of her *galabeya* and try to put her black nipple between his lips. but as soon as she tried to do that the face changed to that of her husband Abdel Moneim. She pushed it back with her hand, but when it looked at her with reproach in its eyes, the features were no longer the same as they had been a moment ago. Now it was Kafrawi's eyes that stared back at her, and filled her heart with a dark panic. A few moments later he had fled behind a door, or a window with iron bars only to return pushing a hand cart in which were piled calves' feet and heads dripping with blood. She could feel her body shrink into her *galabeya*, and would spit*

---

* A common gesture amongst poor women which is supposed to chase devils away.

quickly into its neck then call out to her niece Zeinab. Her eyes kept turning this way and that with a frightened look. When the girl arrived she would say to her, 'Zeinab, my child, do not leave me alone. I am frightened. The devils are looking at me from behind the bars of the window.'

Zeinab looked around but she could see nothing, so she would say to her aunt, 'The window has no iron bars.'

Zakeya would point her trembling fingers to the huge iron door and say, 'It's a window.'

Zeinab's eyes followed her fingers as they pointed to the huge iron gate of the Mayor's house and patted her shoulder. 'It's the door of the Mayor's house. Do not be afraid. Try to get some sleep. I will take the buffalo to the field and come back before sunset.'

Zakeya would catch hold of Zeinab's *galabeya*. 'No, Zeinab, don't leave me alone.'

'But who will go to the field? And who will feed us if I stay here by your side?'

Zakeya answered, 'Galal has taken the buffalo and gone to the field. You stay here with me. Don't leave me alone.'

Zeinab would dry her tears quickly, and say, 'Galal has not gone to the field. I must go to harvest the crop so that we can pay what we owe to the government, otherwise they will take the land away from us, and we will have to beg at people's doors.'

At that moment the voice of a man rang out reaching them across the threshold of their house. 'It's not thinkable that we would let Zakeya and Zeinab be obliged to beg at people's doors. As long as we are here alive in Kafr El Teen this will never happen.'

Zeinab turned round to find Haj Ismail standing in the

doorway in front of her. One eye was looking at her, while his other eye wandered in another direction.

She said, 'Haj Ismail, I have to go to our field and, as you can see, my Aunt Zakeya is sick. She no longer eats, nor drinks, nor does she even sleep. All the time she sees things and hears voices, and it makes her very frightened.'

'Zakeya is possessed by a devil,' said Haj Ismail, 'and it will not leave her unless she listens to my advice, and does what I tell her to do.'

'I am prepared to do anything that will make my Aunt Zakeya get well again, Haj Ismail.'

He opened his old bag and extracted a long piece of paper covered with verses of the Koran. He chanted a few obscure incantations, folded the piece of paper and put it in a small dirty pouch of rough white cotton. Then he hung it around Zakeya's neck, chanting other verses and incantations. After that he muttered a few words and started to invoke the name of God and exalt His unlimited power, all the while stroking her head, her face and her chest first with the palms of his hands and then with their backs.

After finishing he wiped his face in his hands and said to Zeinab, who was now sitting close to her aunt, 'This amulet has great powers. It costs only five piastres. And now, Zeinab, listen carefully to me and do exactly what I tell you. Next Thursday, together with your aunt, you are to take the bus to Bab El Hadeed in Cairo. From Bab El Hadeed you will take the tram to Sayeda Zeinab.* There you will find people celebrating her birth anniversary, groups of people chanting hymns to her

---

* A mosque built in memory of the Prophet Mohamed's daughter Zeinab. *Sayeda* is a term of respect used for women.

memory, and many holy people. Both of you offer a prayer to her soul and join in the chanting. Repeat the names of Allah many times with those who are chanting. and spend your night in the mosque in the bosom of our holy lady. On Friday morning raise your hands to the heavens and say, "O God, O God, listen to me. My Aunt Zakeya asks forgiveness for all her sins and will never do anything to displease You. Have mercy on her, You the all merciful." Allah will lend an ear to your exhortations and a holy man will approach your Aunt Zakeya and take this amulet off her neck, then hang it on her again. While he is doing this he will enjoin her to fulfil certain things. After he has finished she is to give him a ten piastre silver coin. Then both of you should return immediately, and do what he has told you without delay. Remember his words exactly, for what he says to you will be the orders of Allah. If you do not obey, the wrath of Allah will pursue your Aunt Zakeya. and the devil will never leave her body.'

Zeinab looked at him and said in a voice which expressed deep feeling, 'May Allah give you long life, Haj Ismail. I am prepared to take my Aunt to Sayeda Zeinab, and to do anything Allah tells me to do.'

On the eve of Thursday Om Saber came to their house at night, and bathed Zakeya's body with pure water from the river Nile. Zeinab tied the corner of her shawl around the few coins some of the neighbours had collected for them to pay for the bus and tram fares, as well as the five piastres for the amulet and a silver coin of ten piastres which was the price she was supposed to pay in order to know what Allah wanted her to do. Zakeya muttered a few words as though talking to herself, 'Even God wants us to pay Him something. Yet He knows we own nothing, my child.'

And Zeinab answered, 'Do not worry about anything, the good which Allah bestows upon people is without end, and kind people are to be found everywhere. What matters is that Allah should forgive you, and drive the evil spirit out of you.'

# XII

Before the crimson rays of dawn had appeared in the east, before the cock had crowed, or the voice of Sheikh Hamzawi called to prayer, the big wooden door opened creaking with the rusty sound of an ancient water-wheel. Two shadows slipped out, their heads and shoulders draped in long black shawls. Zeinab's face was drawn and pale under the first rays of dawn. She looked up at the sky with an expression of angry defiance. Moving alongside her could be seen the thin, emaciated, lined face of Zakeya, her big black eyes gleaming in the half-light.

Darkness lifted slightly and the light of dawn glimmered over the surface of the river revealing the tiny exhausted waves like wrinkles on an old, sad silent face that has resigned itself to its fate. Fitful gusts of wind blew the dust off the top of the river bank to the slope below, then further down to the lowland where the huts huddled close together, their roofs stacked with piles of dry cotton sticks, dung cakes and straw, their windows tiny holes like eyes that do not see, their doors of roughened wood, their walls made of mud and clay.

But the big house of the Mayor was quite different. Its walls were high and built of red brick, its door rose up menacingly black, with iron bars reaching up to the top, its windows were made of glass and wooden frames, its roof climbed higher than the minaret and no cotton sticks, or straw, or cakes of dung were to be seen on it, for it was made of concrete and always kept spotlessly clean.

They walked with their eyes fixed on the long road which lay ahead, leaving behind them, on the dust of the bank, the imprints of four big feet, each with five toes slightly splayed. Zeinab's imprints were a little smaller and much clearer for in her legs was a greater strength. They struck against her garment with a regular flap. Her eyes gazed along the parallel stretches of water and green crops which reached out as far as the distant horizon. To her they seemed endless, and she wondered where Sayeda Zeinab could be, and where she would find the bus which would carry them to Bab El Hadeed. Zakeya had started to lose her breath. She put her arm around her niece's shoulders, and went silently on without a word of complaint.

At the place where the river curved they came upon a big mulberry tree. There they found an old man and a young woman sitting in its shade. On the ground by their side was a small basket. Zeinab stopped and asked them about the bus. The old man said, 'Yes, my child, wait here with us. We are also going to El Sayeda.'

They sat down on the dusty ground near them, the old man's eyes kept running between them, then he asked, 'My child, is your mother ill?'

Zeinab answered, 'She's my aunt. My mother died many years ago, uncle.'

'May Allah have mercy on her. All of us will die, it's our destiny. But to be sick is another thing. May Allah spare you the misery of being sick.'

Zeinab looked at the young woman sitting by his side. She noticed that her eyes were fixed on something far away, as though she was not interested in what they were saying. She asked the old man, 'Is she your daughter, uncle?'

'No, she's my wife,' he answered. 'She was in good health, but I don't know what happened to her. Almost overnight she started to refuse all food and drink, stayed awake all night, unable to sleep, and got into the habit of talking to herself. She sees things, and screams out in the middle of the night. I took her to one Sheikh after another. They gave her amulets to wear, and we arranged a *zar* for her. I spent all the money I have but nothing worked. So Sheikh Abbas advised me to take her on a pilgrimage to the Hejaz so that she could visit the house of Allah. Allah would forgive her for her sins, and drive away the evil spirit which had entered her body. But I explained to Sheikh Abbas that I was a poor man and had spent all my money on the Sheikhs. I did not have the means to pay for this journey. So he told me to take her to El Sayeda. I would exhort El Sayeda Zeinab to intervene with God on her behalf, and ask Him to forgive her sins. He advised me to take a basket of figs and offer it to El Sayeda. I swear by Allah, my child, that in order to collect the money for this journey I went from house to house begging. Then I bought this basket of figs. And here I am on my way to El Sayeda in the hope that Allah will cure her of her sickness.'

'God is great, my uncle,' said Zeinab. 'He will not abandon her.'

The old man glanced at Zakeya. She was sitting silently with her large black eyes fixed on the horizon as though she was not following what they were saying, or could not hear them. The old man asked, 'Are you taking her to El Sayeda?'

'Yes, uncle,' Zeinab replied.

'Doesn't she have a man to travel with? Don't you have anybody to look after you, my child?'

'We have no one but Allah, and a buffalo which we left behind with our neighbour, Om Soliman. She will feed it in return for the work it will do in her field.'

'God be with you both, my child. May God come to your help, and to the help of all those who need Him.'

Zeinab raised her hands to heaven and said, 'We call upon Thee to stand by our side, O God.'

The disc of the sun climbed higher in the sky. The earth got hotter and hotter, and the air was still. Zeinab rested her head against a tree trunk and closed her eyes to get some sleep, but she woke up suddenly to the noise of the bus. It came to a sudden stop nearby, raising a thick haze of dust. It was leaning heavily on one side as though the slightest touch could make it turn over. Its back was charred and exuded dense clouds of black smoke which mingled with the dust. Zakeya rested her arm on Zeinab as she climbed the steps, and the old man helped his young companion to clamber in. They managed to push their way through, to become a part of the compact mass of bodies and baskets which filled the interior of the bus. They felt themselves enveloped by the hot, stuffy air which seemed to close around them with its load of dust and smoke. Zakeya and the young woman squatted down on the floor amidst the other passengers, near the driver's seat. But the old man and Zeinab remained standing like most of the others. The bus leapt forwards suddenly and Zeinab fell with all the weight of her body on the old man standing behind her, making him lose his balance and land in turn on the passengers standing in the aisle. In less than the wink of an eye those who were upright had fallen on those who were sitting down converting the inside of the bus into layers of compressed air and compact flesh. A moment later the bus started to advance at a slow pace along the summit of the river bank. Those who had fallen down now had a chance to extricate themselves, and stand up, and things returned to normal once more. Zeinab and the old man stood close to one another in the aisle.

The bus continued to reel along carrying its heavy load. The broken windows rattled, and now and again a piece of glass fell off the doors and the chairs seemed to be half-way out of their sockets, and parts were already so loose that they shook with a continuous metallic noise. Since the bus was advancing over a surface which was full of holes and bumps the din was deafening, and it seemed that at any moment it would come apart at its joints. Water kept streaming out between the wheels like urine from an old man who no longer is able to control his bladder and lets it drip down between his tottering legs. The bus was very much like a drunken old sailor swaying and reeling all the way. Puffs of black smoke kept exuding out of it from behind, and at every turn on the river bank it leaned heavily on one side, as though at any moment it might fall into the waters of the Nile. But each time the driver would jump to his feet, haul on the steering wheel with all his might, and save the bus from an imminent catastrophe just in time, only to find it flinging itself to the other side with the obvious intent of descending the slope and landing in the ditch, which at least was completely dry. But the driver, who seemed well-versed in its antics, would repeat the same manoeuvre until the four wheels of the bus touched down on top of the river bank at one time. Then reassured he sat down again, his half-closed eyes on the road, as though there was nothing he longed for more than a chance to shut his lids completely and drop off into a sound sleep while he was driving. His sallow, wizened face stood out with its worn look against the background of turbaned heads, long garments, limbs, and straw or wicker baskets.

Zakeya closed her eyes as she sat on the floor of the bus, overwhelmed by the sight of all these faces, and bodies pressed up so closely against each other. She had never ridden in a bus before, nor seen so many bodies packed into so small a space, nor felt her body shake as violently as it was shaking now. Every now and then a particularly violent leap of the bus would make her open her eyes in fright. She felt that the ground was going to turn upside down and come down on the roof of the bus, or that the bus was going to do a somersault and land with its roof on the road. She kept spitting into the neck of her *galabeya* and muttering the testimony as though for the last time before she died. 'Verily I do witness that there is no Allah except Allah, and that Mohamed is the prophet of Allah.' Many other voices in the bus would echo in her ears, almost gasping in one breath as they repeated the same words over and over again.

At certain moments it would seem to her that she had died, and then come back to life in the bus which continued to ride over the river bank along the Nile. She lifted her head to try and get a glimpse of the river, but the bodies around her obstructed the windows and doors and she could see only the roof of the bus pitch black as though covered with oven soot.

She did not realize that the bus had come to a stop except when she felt Zeinab tug at her hand and say, 'We get down here, Aunt.'

She rested her hands on Zeinab's back and got down from the bus. Her face went very pale, and her eyes seemed to grow even blacker than usual, when she looked around and found neither river, nor river banks, neither mud huts nor muddy lanes, but wide shining streets, huge buildings, cars that raced along one after the other, and trams from which arose a strange clanging, or shrieking noise. The people, too, were different. The women walked along on high heels, and their thighs and breasts were partly exposed by the tight fitting clothes they wore. Gentlemen crowded through the streets in such great numbers that it was difficult to tell how many of them there were. On either side were rows of shops and the movement in the streets was rapid, almost hectic and flowed along unceasingly accompanied by a high-pitched, hectic roar. She held on to Zeinab's hand tightly and pressed her body up as close to her as she could.

'My head's whirling round, Zeinab,' she said. 'Don't leave me. Hold on to my hand. I don't know whether it's my head that's going round all the time, or things around me.'

But Zeinab's head was also in a whirl. Her big black eyes kept looking at what went on around her with a growing amazement. The old man in turn started to lean on Zeinab, while the young woman held on to him tightly. The four of them stood there amidst the flow of passers-by, huddled together for support. Their mouths were gaping in astonishment, and their eyes darted here and there or went round and round with the same frenzied movement as the bustling crowds.

After a while they started to walk along in single file close to a high wall, stepping warily over the ground, overcome by the feeling that as soon as one of their feet touched the ground it would be caught up in one of the churning wheels of the cars which raced up and down. Zeinab asked one of the passers-by where they could find the tram which would take them to El Sayeda. The man pointed to a column rising up from the ground and said, 'Stand here until the tram comes.'

They stood where the man told them. It was a place full of people. When Zeinab looked up she could see long wires stretching overhead above the street. Opposite where they stood was a huge building, and behind the wires was a huge picture which showed a naked woman lying on her back with her legs open, and three men pointing their pistols at her.

She hid her face behind her shawl and said in a low voice, 'Shame on them.'

The people getting on and off the tram kept pushing against one another on the small step which looked as though it could easily give way under the pressure. Zeinab hung on to an iron rail and pulled Zakeya up behind her. Then it was the turn of the young woman, followed by the old man who was hanging on carefully to his basket of figs. But just as he was opening a way for himself, the basket slipped from his shoulder and fell under the wheels of the tram. The old man jumped off after it. Someone screamed, then there were several screams. The figs rolled over the step and were scattered over the asphalt road, to be squashed under the shoes of the people walking along. The conductor quickly blew his whistle and the tram came to a halt.

Zakeya did not see what had happened. She could not tell whether the tram was moving or had come to a stop. She closed her eyes in an attempt to prevent her head from going round and round. When she opened her eyes again her body was shaking with the movement of the tram. Zeinab was sitting next to her, and in front of her was a small window through which she could see the street full of people walking up and down. She could also glimpse the tall buildings on one side. Many of them were covered with huge posters showing almost naked women, lying down, or sitting or standing with their legs apart. In front of them there were always gentlemen and they all carried pistols. She felt that something had happened in the tram, clasped Zeinab's hand tightly by the fingers and enquired, 'What's the matter?'

'The old man,' said Zeinab, 'fell under the wheels of the tram and has gone to the Kasr El Aini Hospital instead of El Sayeda.'

Zakeya gestured with her hand as though pointing to something going on outside the window of the tram way up in the sky. 'Only Allah is all-powerful, my child. Is the world here mad, or is it your Aunt Zakeya who has lost her mind?'

'May Allah make you whole and keep your mind as good as it has always been. Thanks be to Allah you are all right, my Aunt, and Allah will make you even better after you have visited El Sayeda.'

'Blessed you will always be, our lady,' murmured Zakeya.

# XIII

The bodies of Zakeya and Zeinab seemed to become one with the compact mass of human flesh which flowed into El Sayeda Zeinab mosque filling it up and overflowing to the area around, the narrow streets which led to it, the main thoroughfare traversed by the trams that came and went and the big square to which it led. It was a mass composed of human bodies all wearing long *galabeyas*. The women could be distinguished from the men by the black shawls they wore over their heads. The myriad throng walked barefoot, their toes big and flat, their heels dark and cracked, the palms of their hands rough and horny with a groove made in the middle by the hoe, or the plough or the *tambour*. The faces were pale, and drawn, and thin, the eyes black and big, wide open with wonder, or half closed in a kind of stupor or daze, the mouths gaping in one big gasp which took in the air and kept it inside.

Zakeya held on tightly to Zeinab's hand, and she stuck so closely to her that she almost walked in her steps, afraid that the slightest distance between them, even if only a hair's breadth, might lead to her getting lost in this mighty human ocean. But as they moved along somehow people managed to slip between them and in the flash of an eye Zakeya lost sight of Zeinab. Yet for some obscure reason she no longer felt afraid, or alone. Everything around her was now familiar, known, lived before. The *galabeyas* dropping down over people's bodies were like her *galabeya*, and the sweat of their bodies had the same odour as her sweat. The faces, the feet, the toes, the way they walked, and stared and spoke were things she shared in common with them. She was a part of this compact mass of human bodies, and it was like a part of her.

She was no longer afraid and her eyes ceased to search among the crowds for Zeinab. For all the faces she saw were like Zeinab's, and all the voices she heard reminded her of Zeinab's voice. Even the words, the way they pronounced them, their very intonation, the lifting of hands to the heavens, the single unchanging cry, 'O God, come to our rescue, O God' chanted out in one voice, made her feel that all these people were Zeinab.

They were sick or blind. They were young or old. They were children or babes in arms. They were sheikhs of sects, or beggars or thieves. They were sorcerers, and fortune-tellers, people who made amulets or recited religious chants. They were saints of God, intermediaries to His Grace, guardians of the doors to Heaven. All of them like Zakeya and Zeinab raised the palms of their rough hands in one uniform movement to Allah on high and chanted in one voice, in one breath, 'O God.'

Zeinab too had ceased looking for Zakeya. Her face was now only one of the innumerable faces, a drop in the human ocean, a single garment amongst a million robes, an invisible particle in the infinite universe, a pair of hands lifted to the heavens amidst a forest of hands fluttering in the wind, a voice joined to myriad voices in one prolonged, imploring chant, more like a wail of despair than anything else. 'O God, come to our rescue.' The voice of Zakeya too pierced through her lips in a high-pitched shriek which rose from her inner depths, like the cry from a slaughtered neck, or the gasp of a wounded chest.

Zeinab's heart was beating wildly as she cried out 'O God.' It seemed to leap against her ribs, and shake her small breasts under the bodice of her long robe. Her eyes shone with a mysterious gleam like moonlight on a dark, silent stream. She shivered every now and then with a strange fever hidden in her depths, and the blood rose to her face in a virginal flush as though this was the first time her heart had beaten for anyone.

So she cried out 'O God' and with every cry she felt she came closer to Him, so that now He could hear her voice and feel her breath on Him. She, too, could hear His Voice and feel His Breath. Her body had become one with Him, and she shivered with a sudden fear which was more like a deep sorrow, with a feeling of relief more like deep pleasure. She wanted to weep, to shriek with joy, to close her eyes and abandon herself to Him, to savour to the end this feeling of relief, of a body no longer under tension, of a deep pleasure she had never experienced before. But somehow deep inside her there remained a fearful sadness, an exhaustion, an anxiety which prevented her from sleeping, or even from just closing her eyes. So there she sat through the long hours with wide-open staring eyes, almost unaware of what went on around her.

But suddenly she heard someone call out her name, 'Zeinab!' She realized at once that it was the voice of God. She had called out to Him all through the night and now He was calling out to her in turn. She whispered 'O God' and He answered 'Zeinab.' She moved towards the voice as though in a dream. She did not know whether she was walking on legs, or flying on wings. The compact mass of bodies around her, the myriad voices resounding in her ears fell back, and disappeared, leaving an empty space in which echoed one voice calling out 'Zeinab.' She saw a face emerge in front of her from what might have been a thick mist, or a dense cloud of smoke. It was not the face of a man, nor that of a woman. It was not the face of a young child or of an old person. It was a face without sex or age, like that of Om Saber. Instead of the black shawl she wore, the head was covered in a huge white turban which reached down midway to the eyebrows concealing the dark pitted skin over the upper half of the forehead. The skin of the face also was blotched and pitted as though the old smallpox had left its marks. The eyes were small without lashes, or even lids. Just two dark holes staring unmovingly at Zeinab.

'Are you Zeinab, daughter of Kafrawi?' the voice said.

She gasped out a frightened 'Yes.' Deep inside her another voice asked, 'How did he recognize me amidst all these people?' But another voice replied almost immediately, 'Praise be to Allah, for He knows all things.'

'Where is your aunt, Zakeya?' asked the man.

And the voice echoed inside her again. 'He also knows that my aunt's name is Zakeya. It's amazing...'

She looked round trying to find out where her aunt had gone. She could see her nowhere. But after a short while she realized that Zakeya's hand was still tightly clasped around hers, and that her shivering body was pressed closely up against her. She could hear her muttering verses and words under her breath.

The man came close to Zakeya, put out his dark, gnarled hand to the neck of her *galabeya*, took hold of the amulet she was wearing between his fingers, and took it off her neck. He recited a few verses, paused for a moment, and then put it back around her neck. Zakeya followed what he was doing intently, with an expression of deep reverence in her eyes, as though she was about to kneel and prostrate herself at his feet. As soon as his hand was still, she bent over and pressed her lips to it with a passionate fervour, muttering to herself. The man abandoned his dark, gnarled hand to her, and turned to Zeinab.

'Your aunt Zakeya is sick. She is sick because you have continued to disobey Allah, and she has encouraged you to do that. But Allah is all merciful, and kind, and He will forgive both of you on condition that you obey, and do what He asks of you. He will cure her of all sickness, if He so will, blessed be His Name on high.'

They raised their hands to the heavens and chanted in one breath, 'We thank, and praise Thee. For Thou art the generous and the bountiful one, O God.'

'You are to spend the night in the bosom of El Sayeda,' said the man. 'Then tomorrow before dawn you are to start out for Kafr El Teen. There bathe yourselves with clean water from the Nile, and while you wash continue to recite the testimony. Once dressed you should do your prayers. Start with the four ordained prostrations, then follow them with the four *Sunna* prostrations. After that you are to repeat the holy verse of the *Seat* ten times. On the following day, before dawn, Zeinab is to take another bath with clean water from the Nile, meanwhile repeating the testimony three times. Then do her prayer at the crack of dawn. Once this is over she is to open the door of your house before sunrise, stand on the threshold facing its direction and recite the first verse of the Koran ten times. In front of her she will see a big iron gate. She is to walk towards it, open it and walk in. She must never walk out of it again until the owner of the house orders her to do so. He is a noble and great man, born of a noble and great father, and he belongs to a good and devout family blessed by Allah and His Prophet. During this time Zakeya should lead the buffalo to the field, tie it to the water-wheel, take her hoe and work until the call to noon prayers. As soon as she hears it she should put down her hoe and pray the four ordained prostrations, followed by the four *Sunna* prostrations. After her prayers are over she must remain in the kneeling position and recite the opening verse of the Koran ten times, then raise her hands to the heavens, and repeat "Forgive me, O God" thirty times. As soon as she is over with this she is to get up, and wipe her face in the palms of her hand, and, God willing, she will find herself completely cured.'

Zakeya bent low over the dark gnarled hand and pressed her lips to it fervently, as she whispered, 'I do thank and praise Thee, O God. I do thank and praise Thee, O God.'

While this was going on Zeinab had kept repeating verses of praise and thanks to God. She was so overcome with holy bliss that she forgot to give the man the ten piastre coin as Haj Ismail had instructed her to do. But the man himself now asked her for it. She undid the knotted corner of her shawl with a hand which was still trembling, extracted the coin, gave it to him and kissed his hand as though she was making the offering to God. Deep inside her a voice kept whispering in wonderment, 'O God, he knows Kafr El Teen and our house, and the iron gate which stands in front of it.'

The man disappeared into the crowd as rapidly as he had emerged, leaving Zakeya and Zeinab standing where they were, huddled up against each other in a state of wonderment, and profound humility. Now and again they would look at one another questioningly, as though to reassure themselves that what had happened was real, and not a figment of their imagination, that they had really heard the voice of God, and even seen Him, or at least seen one of His messengers, or saints to whom had been revealed the secrets which were not revealed to others. Zakeya felt her body was now lighter than it had ever been before. The iron grasp which seemed to throttle her all the time had loosened a little. She no longer had to lean on her niece Zeinab, for her legs had regained their strength, and could carry her easily.

Zeinab's eyes became wider and wider with amazement when she noticed her aunt walking beside her as though she could easily manage on her own.

'Aunt, you are better already,' she said in a low voice, full of reverence. 'Look how you are walking!'

And the old woman responded, 'My body no longer feels heavy. O God, verily Thou art generous and bountiful.'

'God is great,' said Zeinab. 'Did I not tell you many a time that Allah would help us, and that you should pray to Him, and be patient?'

'Yes, my child, you always used to say that to me.'

'I disobeyed God and refused to pray, and so did you, Aunt Zakeya.'

'I did not refuse to pray. It was the evil spirit dwelling within which refused.'

'God willing the evil spirit will be driven out of your body when we do what He has ordained.'

'Do you remember all that the sheikh said?' asked Zakeya. 'My body kept shaking, and I am unable to recall his words. I'm afraid we might forget something.'

'Don't worry about anything. Every word he said is engraved here in my heart.'

'May God bless you,' said Zakeya fervently.

# XIV

And so that morning before dawn, Zeinab lifted the earthenware jar high up and poured clean Nile water from it over her head and body. She rubbed her breasts with it, whispering 'I testify that there is no Allah except Allah, and that Mohamed is the prophet of Allah' three times. The water flowed down over her belly and thighs, and she rubbed them in turn, reciting the testimony three times. She dried her long, black hair, plaited it tightly, dressed in a clean *galabeya*, wound the black shawl around her head and shoulders and advanced with frightened, hesitant steps towards the door, before pushing it slowly wide open.

The crimson rays of dawn started to appear above the horizon but the sun had not yet risen in the sky. She fixed her eyes on the spot from which she knew it would rise, and read the first verse of the Koran in a soft voice, repeating it ten times. Then she walked towards the iron gate. She was still frightened, but now her steps were steady, very steady. When she arrived at the gate a shiver went through her body. It was no longer a shiver of fear or doubt, but of deep exaltation. Now she knew what it was that she had to do. Her heart beat fast, her chest breathed full, her body was taut with expectation. Her legs trembled under the long *galabeya* and her large black eyes were raised to the sky, watching for something extraordinary to appear, for the will of God to be fulfilled.

The blue eyes of the Mayor opened wide with wonderment when he saw her appear. From her face and her eyes, from the way she walked with her head held high, he realized at once that she was Zeinab. He rubbed his eyes and looked at her again speaking in a voice which expressed surprise.

'Who sent you, Zeinab?'

'It is Allah Who has sent me,' she said.

'But why did you come this time?'

'Because it is the will of God,' she said as though speaking to herself.

The Mayor smiled, got out of bed and went to the bathroom. He brushed his teeth, washed, then looked at his face in the mirror and smiled again. The laughter was welling up inside him. Speaking to himself in an undertone, he said, 'Devil, son of a devil. What a cunning rogue you are, Haj Ismail!'

When he had finished he came out of the bathroom, and started to look for his watch. He found it on a small table. Its hands were pointing to six o'clock. He grinned and whispered to himself, 'No woman has ever come to me so early in the morning. I must drink a cup of tea first. It will wake me up.'

Zeinab was still standing where he had left her. He walked up to her, and in a voice one would use when speaking to a child, said, 'Listen to me, Zeinab. I want a cup of tea. Do you know how to make tea?'

'Yes, my master,' she said in a tone of voice anxious to please.

'Come with me. I will show you the way to the kitchen. I want you to prepare tea for me while I have a bath.'

Zeinab gasped in wonder when she saw the white porcelain wash basins, the shining metal taps, the coloured walls, the curtains and the stove that lit so easily. She lost herself in contemplation of the kettle which blew a whistle when the water boiled, the cups with engravings and coloured paintings, the silver spoons. Everything around her was new, never seen before, as though she had been transported to another world. She felt that she was now in the kingdom of Allah, praised be His name and revered. Her fingers trembled every time she held something between them. Her heart was beating rapidly, her breast heaved up and down, and her legs kept shaking all the time.

A tea-cup slipped through her fingers and dropped on the floor. She clapped her hand over her chest and shrank to the wall breathing hard, her eyes fixed on the shattered fragments of the cup as though she had committed a terrible crime. The pieces of porcelain shone like coloured crystals over the milk-white floor. The Mayor was enjoying his warm shower when he heard the sound of the cup as it struck the ground followed by a loud, terrified gasp. He smiled as his hand rubbed slowly over his chest and belly with a cake of perfumed soap. He thought, 'How exciting these simple girls are, and how pleasant it is to take their virgin bodies into one's arms, like plucking a newly opened rose flower. How I hate the false sophistication of Cairo women, like my wife with her brazen eyes. Nothing any longer intimidates or thrills her. Her frigid body no longer quivers when I caress her, or hold her tight, or even bite her.'

He came out of the bathroom wearing pink silk pyjamas and walked to the kitchen. He found Zeinab still standing shrunk up against the wall, with her hand on her breast, her lips slightly parted as though she were out of breath, and her eyes fixed on the shattered fragments of porcelain which just a moment ago had been a beautiful cup worth much more than she would ever know.

He watched her thoughtfully with his clear blue eyes, his face looking relaxed and healthy, just as though he were carefully weighing a priceless ornament. Her thick black hair hung in two plaits over her back. She had a fine, oval face tanned by the sun and her timidity was so stimulating, it excited him. Her full lips were a natural red, and slightly moist like a flower in the morning dew. Her breasts were round, firm, upturned with the sharp outlines of healthy flesh. They rose and fell in continuous movement as though impelled by the racing heart which hid behind them. Her eyes were large and black with a trace of tears like a child who has taken fright.

He came close to her and said with a smile on his lips, 'Are you crying, Zeinab?'

She bent her head and answered in a barely audible whisper, 'It fell out of my hand. Forgive me, master.'

She wiped her tears away with her hand. He felt the blood surge up in his body and moved closer, stretching out his hand and tenderly wiping away the remaining tears.

'Do not be afraid, Zeinab,' he said in a low voice. 'The cup, and the owner of the cup, are all yours.'

He was about to take her in his arms but thought better of it. She might only become more frightened if he did that. It was better if he waited until she had become accustomed to her new surroundings, and all the things she was seeing for the first time.

During that time Zakeya had taken the buffalo to the field, tied it to the water-wheel, and started to dig deep into the ground with her hoe. She kept straining her ears to catch a sound even vaguely resembling the midday call to prayer. When the voice of Sheikh Hamzawi finally rang out, the disc of the sun was right over her head, burning down on it, and the sweat poured in a continuous flow, welling out from the roots of her hair, down her neck, and over her back, and her chest. She could feel it trickling down between her thighs and wondered whether it was sweat, or the urine she could no longer keep in her bladder. As soon as the call to prayer died out, she threw her hoe aside, and went to a nearby stream. She washed her face and neck and did her ablutions, then stood on the edge of the stream to pray, kneeling down and prostrating herself with a fervent devotion. She did the four ordained prostrations and followed them with the four *Sunna* prostrations. With her prayers over she remained kneeling, and recited the first verse of the Koran ten times. After that she raised her hands to the heavens and repeated, 'O God, forgive me,' thirty times. She paused for a moment before wiping her face in her hands. Immediately she experienced a strange feeling of relief, very much like a strong desire to sleep. Her lids grew heavy and in a moment she fell into a deep sleep beside the stream.

No matter how burning hot the noonday sun became it could never penetrate through the thick, solid concrete walls of the Mayor's house. Nevertheless the Mayor felt waves of burning heat running through his body as though he were naked under a white hot sun. He was still wearing his pink silk pyjamas, and sat in the armchair reading his morning newspaper. He glimpsed his brother's picture on one of the pages; quickly turned it over and started to read the news about celebrities and society people. Thus he learnt that Touha the dancer had been divorced, that Noussa the actress was marrying for the fourth time, and that

Abdel Rahman, the singer, had entered the hospital to have his appendix removed. He turned over the page to read the sports news, but the pages got stuck, and he found himself looking at his brother's picture again, so he ran over the lines and read that there had been a cabinet change, and that his brother had become an even more important minister. He clicked his tongue in derision. No one knew him better than he did, for he was his brother. And no one knew how stupid a man he was, so slow of understanding, but a real mule for work 'just like a buffalo which goes round and round in a water-wheel with its eyes blindfolded', he thought.

He let the paper fall from his hand and closed his eyes, but suddenly remembered that he wanted to telephone his wife, and ask her how his younger son had fared in the examinations. His hand was about to reach out to the telephone when he heard the sound of water being poured in the bathroom. It reminded him that Zeinab had come to his house at dawn, and that meanwhile she had swept and cleaned the house, so that now all that remained for her to do was the bathroom. A thought flashed through his mind. 'Why not go to the bathroom and have a try?' But he drove it away. Somehow he felt that Zeinab was not like her sister Nefissa who was simple and easy-going, and had not instilled in him the same caution and hesitation he felt in the presence of Zeinab. He could not understand why with Zeinab he was so cautious and hesitant, even afraid. Yes, afraid. Perhaps because she was Nefissa's sister. True, Nefissa's story had remained a secret, but who knew? Maybe this time things would not be concealed so easily. He tried to chase away his fears. Who could find out the things that had happened? He was above suspicion, above the law, even above the moral rules which governed ordinary people's behaviour. Nobody in Kafr

El Teen would dare suspect him. They could have doubts about Allah, but about him... It was impossible.

But now he remembered that there were three men in Kafr El Teen who knew almost everything about him. The Chief of the Village Guard, the Sheikh of the mosque, and the village barber. Without them he could not rule Kafr El Teen. They were his instruments, his aides and his means for administering the affairs of the village. But they knew his secrets. They could be trusted to keep them, although deep down inside he felt that they were not to be trusted with anything. If he closed his eyes for a single second they would play a trick on him, or get out of him whatever they could. But he had his eyes wide open, and he knew how to convince them that he could hear them breathe as they slept, and that if any one of them even so much as thought of playing tricks, of wagging his tail, he would cut it off for him, and cut his head off with it, too.

He swallowed two or three times in quick succession. His mouth was bitter and he felt like spitting, like ridding himself of the hatred which for ever weighed down on him. He loathed the three men, and despised them. What made it even worse was the realization that he needed them, that he could not do without them. That was why he was obliged to spend some of his nights talking and joking and laughing with them, and even to convince himself not only that they were his friends, but perhaps his only friends.

He got up from his comfortable armchair, walked to the bathroom and spat into the wash basin, then gargled with water several times trying to rid his mouth of the bitter taste. He looked in the mirror and his eyes fastened themselves on the reflection of Zeinab scrubbing the bath tub so that it shone as clean as alabaster. Her long *galabeya* was wet, and had stuck to her body revealing her breasts and thighs. It was as though she was naked before his eyes. He felt the warm blood rush to his belly and he could no longer take his eyes off her young body.

Zeinab lifted her head bent over the bath and stood upright. She caught the blue eyes of the Mayor fastened on her with a strange look, and stepped back in a movement of fear, shrinking up against the wall as though seeking protection. But her foot slipped on the smooth wet tiles, and in a moment she was lying full length on the floor.

Before she had time to rest her hands on it for support and get up, his arm was already round her waist helping her to rise. The tips of his fingers brushed against her breast, and he felt his hand tremble as it moved stealthily around its smooth contour until it was cupped in his palm.

She gave a half-throttled shriek, part pain at the hard pressure of his hand around her breast sensitive with youth and inexperience, part fright running through her body with an icy shiver, and part pleasure, a strange new pleasure almost akin to an ecstasy, the ecstasy of salvation, of being free of the heavy load which had been weighing down on her heart. Now she could leave herself in the hands of God, deliver her body and soul to Him, fulfil her vow, and savour the relief of having done so.

His hand moved up her legs, lifted the wet garment over her thighs. She heard his voice, hoarse, its tone low and tense with desire whispering in her ear, 'Take off your *galabeya*, Zeinab, otherwise you will catch cold.'

His hands were now sliding up her thighs to her belly as he tried to lift her garment higher. But it was wet and stuck to her flesh. He pulled on it so hard that it split with a rending sound. She gasped, 'My *galabeya*! It's my only *galabeya*!'

He tore the remaining folds from around her body, held her tight, whispering in her ear, 'I will buy you a thousand *galabeyas*.'

He stretched out his hand, opened the tap and a shower of warm water poured down over her naked body. With his own hands he washed off the dust and dirt of the day's work, his hands diligent over her hair, her shoulders, her belly, and thighs and breasts.

He dried her in a soft towel smelling of jasmine, the way a mother would dry her child. She let him carry her to the bed, still and silent. Then he took her in his arms.

# XV

Just before the crow of the cock rose into the air, Sheikh
Hamzawi opened his eyes. In fact his eyes had probably
been open for some time taking in the scene which he saw every
day, and wondered at with a wonder that was not pure, and un-
adulterated and innocent but shot through and through with
doubt, with a gnawing, aching, never-ending doubt. Yet the
doubt itself had a strange quality about it, for most of the time,
it was not really doubt, but a deep unshakeable certitude almost
bordering on faith that what he saw before his eyes was an indis-
putable truth, like the truth of the existence of God.

The thin, long finger of dawn crept through a crack in the
window and touched the face of Fatheya with an obscure gleam
of light. It fell on the half of her face to his side, dim, grey,
ashen-like. Her eyes were slightly open as though she were
seeing even in her sleep. Her nose rose in sharp lines, and her
lips were tightly closed together as though she feared that something might pass through them while she slept. The grey light of
dawn revealed her smooth white neck. It ran down to a smooth

white breast welling out where he had unbuttoned her garment over the chest. The child held on to it with its hands, and its lips, and its tightly clenched jaws. She hugged the little body closely in the curve of her arm, with a hold which was tense, as though she feared that some force would tear him away.

Sheikh Hamzawi's look remained fastened to the side of the face he could see with a feeling somewhere between surprise and bewilderment. Was this side of her face so different from the side which the light had not yet reached, and where he would find the features of her face which he knew? What was the difference between the two? He was sure that the features revealed by the light of the dawn were not those of his wife Fatheya. In fact they did not resemble her at all. The nose was her nose, the mouth was her mouth, the neck her neck, the breast was her breast, everything was hers, and yet something had changed, something important but undefinable. He did not doubt for a moment that the woman lying by his side was Fatheya, and that this woman was his wife. He was absolutely sure of this truth, as sure of it as he was of the existence of Allah. And this certitude added to his bewilderment.

Anyone seeing his face at this particular moment would have realized that the man was no longer sure about anything. His eyes were wide open in a fixed stare but near them a small muscle seemed to twitch. The light of dawn pierced through the window and fell on his face. It looked deathly pale and there was a long shadow below it so that the one face looked like two faces. The upper face was his real face, the one which everyone in Kafr El Teen knew. But below it was another face which no one knew, or would ever know because no such face had ever been seen in Kafr El Teen before. It was not the face of a human being, nor that of a spirit. It could have been the face of an angel or a devil, or even the face of Allah, if anyone had seen it before and could recognize Allah's face when he saw it.

Yet as he lay there, Sheikh Hamzawi was feeling further away from God than he had ever felt before. There were moments when he was very close to Allah, and particularly during the Friday midday prayer when all the men of the village, including the Mayor, would stand behind him, perfectly still, unable to move an arm, or a hand, or a finger, unable to move their lips, or whisper a verse from the Koran until he had done so himself.

At such moments he would feel much closer to Allah than any other man amongst them, be it the Mayor himself. A fine shiver would traverse his body, like the fine thrill of pleasure or of that rare happiness which he had known only as a child on those occasions when he used to throw stones at the other children and watch them run away in fright. During the prayer he would deliberately take his time before standing up, or sitting, or kneeling. Now and again he would shoot a quick backward glance, and observe the Mayor and the rows of men assembled behind him, reverently waiting for the slightest movement of his head, or his hand or even his little finger.

Nevertheless, no matter how much he took his time, or even slowed down the prayer, it would still be over in a matter of minutes, and the men would disperse from around him. Some of them might even tread on his foot as they rushed hurriedly behind the Mayor, carrying an appeal or a complaint of some sort written on a sheet of white paper with the required excise duty stamps stuck in the corner. Under his breath he would curse the 'band of impious rascals' who had no respect for God, and were so busy running after the transient panoply of the earth instead of thinking of the life hereafter. He walked back to his home, a lonely figure, stick tapping on the ground, his yellow-beaded rosary swaying between his trembling fingers. His fingers would tremble even more nervously as soon as he spotted his wife Fatheya. He would call out to her, asking for something in a loud throaty voice calculated to sound more throaty and virile than usual, then cough and clear his chest several times to ensure that the neighbours would realize that Fatheya's husband, the man of the household, was back.

'You've become deaf and blind since that accursed child came to our house. He occupies your whole life, and you care about nothing else despite the fact that he is a child born in sin. I held out a merciful hand to him, but sometimes I wish I had left him to die out there. Ever since the accursed creature, fruit of fornication and sin, has come into our house one misfortune after another has befallen us. People blame me for taking him in, their tongues keep wagging and I have lost the respect I used to enjoy in Kafr El Teen. Even my friends have abandoned me, and the Mayor no longer invites me to spend an evening with him. He has advised me several times to send him to a home for illegitimate children. I've promised to do it, but you refuse all the time. I can't understand why you are so attached to this miserable child.'

His voice would tail off as soon as he had asked this question. He did not understand why she should be so enamoured of the child. As soon as he had thrown the question at her, the rosary would begin to tremble even more violently between his fingers, as though he in fact knew the reason, but would not admit it. But it was a knowing devoid of certitude, a kind of obscure suspicion of knowing what one knew without at the same time being sure of it. The knowing and the doubt went through his body with a deep shiver, as though an icy shaft of wind was dropping down from the crack in the window together with the light of dawn.

He could see Fatheya's face, her neck, and the smooth round breast to which the child held so tightly. And the question would start to steal up to him again and crawl over him like the cold, smooth belly of a snake. 'How was her breast giving milk if she had not been pregnant with the child, nor given birth to it?' He had not been the first one to ask this question. He had heard it from somebody else. He could not remember who it was that had asked him. In fact, he was sure it had been a question. Now he thought of it he could recall that it had been just a passing remark pronounced with a whisper. The whisper had made it feel like a sharp knife stabbed into his heart. 'Is Fatheya suckling the child?' He tried to deny that she was suckling it, for he had not seen the child at her breast. Every morning she used to buy buffalo milk for it. But the whispering voice insisted, sure of what it said, with a sureness which brooked no denial.

Sheikh Hamzawi's ears caught the whisper every time he walked along one of the lanes and passed by a group of people. He could see their heads come closer and hear it when it started. He would solemnly pronounce the usual greeting, 'Peace be with you.' Some of them did not even answer. When he passed in front of the shop of Haj Ismail where the Mayor would be seated, surrounded by the Chief of the Village Guard, the village barber and other men, his voice would resound as he said, 'Peace be with you.' There would be a short silence before the answer came back in a low, cold, inconsequential tone, 'And peace be with you.' The voice which answered was not that of the Mayor, nor the village barber. It was some other man who answered. No one among those who were seated invited him to join them. He would return home, walking with his head bowed to the ground to find Fatheya hugging the child. A strong urge to wrench it out of her arms, and throw it out of the window seized him, but each time he would restrict himself to glaring in the direction of the child as though facing a rival so formidable that he did not know how to tackle him.

One night he remained awake until Fatheya fell asleep. He crept on his toes to where the child was lying by her side, and tried to lift it, but although she was fast asleep she held her arms tightly around it. The child as usual was clamped to her breast. She felt him pulling at it and shrieked, 'Shame on you, Sheikh Hamzawi. You are a man of God. He's a small, innocent child.'

'I do not want a child born in sin to remain in my house.'

'Then I will leave the house with him,' she said.

'You are not his mother, and you shall not leave with him.' His voice trembled as he spoke.

'I will not abandon him to the care of anyone else. People have no mercy in their hearts and he's an innocent child who has done no wrong.'

'This child born of sin will bring nothing but trouble to us,' said Sheikh Hamzawi. 'Since he was brought into our home one misfortune after another has happened to us, and to the whole village. The worm has eaten the crops in the fields and I've heard people say he is the cause. No one greets me when I walk along, Fatheya, and I fear the Mayor may chase me out of the mosque and appoint another sheikh in my place. Someone has put into his head the idea that the men of the village no longer like me to lead the prayer, because their prayers might not be favourably received by God since the man who leads them has sheltered a child born of sin and fornication in his house. We will die of hunger, Fatheya, if the Mayor expels me from the mosque.'

'Allah will care for us, Sheikh Hamzawi, if the Mayor chases you out of the mosque,' said Fatheya.

'Allah is not going to make the heavens pour manna on us.'

'How can you of all people say such things about God, Sheikh Hamzawi? Don't you always say that Allah cares for the poor who worship Him? Why would He not take care of us also if the Mayor expels you from the mosque? Have you no trust in Allah, O Sheikh? Have you despaired of His mercy, you who enjoin people never to lose faith? Get up, Sheikh Hamzawi, and do your ablutions and pray God that He may have mercy on you and me, and on all the people in this village.'

So he did his ablutions and prayed. After prayer he would sit on the prayer carpet and recite verses from the Koran. The child would crawl up, sit in front of him on the carpet and look at him with questioning eyes. But the eyes of Sheikh Hamzawi were so full of hatred that they scared him, and he would crawl away screaming at the top of his voice. Fatheya would run up, lift him in her arms and pat him. 'What's the matter, my sweet one, what's the matter with you? Are you afraid of your father, Sheikh Hamzawi? Do not be afraid of him, my sweet one. He's your father and he loves you, and when you grow a little older, he will teach you the Koran, and you will become the Sheikh of the mosque, just like he is. You'll lead people in prayer and give them a sermon on Fridays.'

'You're dreaming, Fatheya,' snorted Sheikh Hamzawi. 'Do you think people here would accept that the Sheikh of the mosque be a man who was born in sin?'

'But it's not the child's fault,' she retorted with insistence.

'I know it's not the child's fault, but people here do not think that way.'

'Why?' she asked. 'Why shouldn't they think the way we do? We're no different to them.'

'Yes, I know, but people are like the waves of the sea, one can never tell when they might become stormy and why. All of them without exception say to me that it's not the child's fault. But when their heads get together, they say something else. These people are unbelievers, Fatheya. They don't have faith in God nor do they worry their heads about what will happen either in this world, or in the next. In their hearts they don't fear God. What they really fear is the Mayor. He holds their daily bread in his hands and if he wants, he can deprive them of it. If he gets angry their debts double, and the government keeps sending them one summons after the other. "Either pay or your land will be confiscated." You do not know the Mayor, Fatheya. He's a dangerous man, and fears no one, not even Allah. He can do injustice to people and put them in gaol when they have done nothing to merit it. He can even murder innocent people.'

'In the name of Allah the Almighty, why then did you keep repeating that he is a man who believes in Allah, and loves doing good to people. Every Friday morning I could hear your voice echoing in the mosque so loudly that it reached me as you made your sermon to the people gathered there, praying to Allah that he bestow long life on the Mayor, saying that he was the best Mayor we had ever had in Kafr El Teen, and that he always sought for truth and justice. Were you fooling people, Sheikh Hamzawi?'

There was a long silence before he replied, 'You know nothing about what goes on outside the four walls of this house. Life in the outside world with people as they are is not easy. The prophet says to us, "Do in this world as though you will live for ever." The Friday sermon, Fatheya, cannot solely be concerned with Allah. Part of it must deal with worldly affairs, and the world in which we live is controlled by the Mayor. We cannot go about our lives if we are in disfavour with him. As far as Paradise is concerned, I am sure that Allah will send me there. Is it not enough that I continue to suffer at the hands of the Mayor and the Chief of the Village Guard in order to protect an innocent child? Or what do you think, Fatheya?'

'Yes, of course,' she said hastily, 'Allah will reward you with many good things because you have adopted an innocent child, and for the protection, tenderness, and care you have given it.'

Taking advantage of the Sheikh's more favourable mood, she sat down next to him and put the child in his lap.

'Look into his eyes, Sheikh Hamzawi. Don't you see how he loves you? Just like a child would love its father. Hold his hand. See how small and soft it is, and how his tiny fingers curl around your thumb as though he's trying to say to you, "Don't leave me father. I am small and weak, and need your help".'

And the child held out its hand and touched Hamzawi's face. The old man bowed his head, abandoning himself submissively to the playful fingers, enjoying their touch as they moved over his whiskers and beard.

One day the child pulled out a hair from his whiskers. He hit him over the hand and said, 'Shame on you.' And so when the boy learnt to speak the first word he pronounced was 'Ame.' The Sheikh began to seat him on the prayer carpet and to teach him how to recite from the Koran. The little boy would try to lift the Koran but it was heavy, and one day it slipped between his hands on to the floor with a thump. Sheikh Hamzawi shook with anger and bent down quickly to lift the Koran from the floor. He kissed it on one side, turned it over and kissed it on the other, then hit the boy on his hand, saying, 'How dare you throw Allah's book on the ground, you son of sin.' Fatheya came running out at the sound of the child's scream, and when the Sheikh explained to her what had happened she said, 'How can you expect him to understand what you're talking about, Sheikh Hamzawi?'

On another occasion it was noonday and very hot. Sheikh Hamzawi was seated as normal with the Koran in his hands, reading passages from it. Sleep overcame him and the Koran dropped on his lap as he sat cross-legged. The small boy crawled up to him and sat on the Koran. A few moments later Sheikh Hamzawi was awakened by something warm and wet trickling down between his thighs. He opened his eyes with a start, thinking that he had urinated on himself, to find the child sitting on his lap. Underneath was the book of Allah all soggy and wet. He scrambled up suddenly, throwing the child off his lap on to the floor, kicked him in the belly and shouted angrily. 'Dost thou pass water on the holy book of Allah, thou son of fornication?'

The boy went pale and could hardly breathe for a moment, as though he was going to choke, or had died suddenly. Then he gave a long wailing gasp which brought Fatheya running up in a terrible panic.

'What happened, Sheikh Hamzawi? What have you done to the child?' she cried out.

Sheikh Hamzawi told her what had happened in a voice which shook with anger. She lifted the child in her arms and screamed furiously at her husband. 'Do you expect the child to realize all this? How can you kick him like that in the belly with your big clumsy foot? Were it not for the grace of Allah you could have killed him!'

'I wish he would die and relieve me of all the suffering I am obliged to go through because of him. I can't stand living in this world any more if this accursed creature is going to continue living in it with me. I'm confined to these four walls like any woman. Nobody visits me any more, and I can no longer visit anybody. And when I walk through the village, people avoid me so that they are not obliged to greet me, or to stop and talk to me.'

On the following Friday Sheikh Hamzawi walked out of his house as usual on his way to the mosque, where he was supposed to lead the congregation in prayer. When he approached the door of the mosque three men stood in his way, and prevented him from entering. He got very angry and shouted at them, 'I am the Sheikh of the mosque. How dare you prevent me from going in?'

'You are no longer the Sheikh of the mosque,' replied one of the men. 'The Mayor has ordered that your services be dispensed with, and has appointed another sheikh.'

'No one can stop me from going in,' shouted Sheikh Hamzawi angrily. 'Allah alone is the one who can prevent me from entering this mosque.' Then he marched straight towards the door. But one of the men held on to his caftan, and pulled him back, upon which he raised his stick and dealt him a heavy blow on the head. The man dropped to the ground immediately, while the other men leapt on Sheikh Hamzawi. One of them struck out at his head with a powerful fist as though he was hitting at the head of a devil, or a snake, while the other man dealt him one slap after the other on the face. He seemed to be taking something out on him, perhaps remembering how his father used to slap him when he was still a young child and say, 'Allah will burn you in the flames of hell for not obeying your father.' The face in front of him now was not that of Sheikh Hamzawi, but of his father. But after a little while it changed again to become the face of Allah who had threatened him as a child that the fire of hell would burn his skin until nothing of it was left, and told him that each time it burnt he would allow another skin to grow on his body so he could burn again once

and twice and thrice and ten and twenty times, never endingly.
When he saw the face of Allah before him he was seized with a
deep panic which made him lash out at Sheikh Hamzawi with
a redoubled fury.

The villagers who had gathered to attend the prayer, crowded
around instead to watch the fight. One of them tried to extricate
Sheikh Hamzawi from the blows raining on his head, but a heavy
fist aimed at his face drove him back, and nearly knocked out
his teeth. He retreated muttering angrily, 'He who tries to stop
a quarrel only gets his clothes torn to shreds.'

One of the men standing around whispered in another's ear,
'The Mayor has removed Sheikh Hamzawi from his job and
appointed another sheikh in the mosque. Come, let's go before
we miss the prayer.' When he moved off others followed, and
as they walked along different thoughts flitted through their
minds. Some of them heard a voice within them say, 'Since the
decision has come from high up, I have no right to oppose it.'
With others, the inner voice said, 'They're all the same, these
sheikhs, so what difference does it make? All I can do is pray
behind one or the other.'

Only a few men remained outside the mosque. They forgot
all about the Friday morning prayer. As a matter of fact, they
forgot almost everything else at the sight of the quarrel. They
stood there enjoying the spectacle of men fighting, not caring
who was doing the beating and who was being beaten as though
both aspects gave them an equal enjoyment. It was the peculiar
pleasure that men experience at watching a violent struggle
between opposing parties, be they human beings, or cocks, or
bulls. Some people are even prepared to pay a high price just
to watch a fight, and be distracted from the conflicts that go
on inside them.

Sheikh Hamzawi's turban fell on the ground and was trodden under the feet of people coming and going. His caftan was now torn to shreds, and blood flowed from his mouth and nose. But he continued to shout out furiously, 'You impious unbelievers. You people who know not Allah. Is that how you strike at the man of God who devoted his life to serving Him all his life, and to looking after His holy house?'

One of the bystanders said, 'If he is the man of God, why does Allah not come to his rescue, instead of leaving him to be beaten up like this?'

'Who said he is a man of God? He is not a man of God at all,' remarked a second.

A third man intervened in defence of the Sheikh, 'How do you know that he is not a man of God? I think he is undoubtedly a man of God.'

'And how are you so sure that he is a man of Allah? I say he is not the man of Allah you say he is,' retorted the second man in an angry voice. But one of the men standing there intervened in the discussion in a way that cut them both short. 'Neither you nor he can tell whether he is a man of God, or not.'

'Then who knows?' asked a man who had been in the thick of the fight just a moment ago.

Another of the bystanders chipped in, 'The Mayor certainly knows. The Mayor is the only one that knows.'

There was a profound silence. No one dared object to what the last man had said. But a small boy who was standing somewhere in the throng piped in a shrill voice, 'How can the Mayor know?' But before he could say anything more, the hand of his father clapped down over his mouth and his hoarse voice ordered, 'Shut your mouth, boy, when there are grown-up men present.'

But the boy's question kept resounding in the mind of one of those who was present. 'Could it be Allah who told the Mayor about such things? But did Allah speak to the Mayor the way he had spoken at one time to the Prophet Mohamed, God's blessing and peace be upon him? Perhaps Allah spoke to saints, and therefore spoke to the Mayor who was a devout man.'

Suddenly the man felt his breath come in gasps. He could not figure out why he had started to gasp since he was only standing like the others watching the fight. Somehow the voice which had spoken within him sounded strange and even frightening, although it had only told him that the Mayor was a devout man. And yet the word devout itself had echoed inside him very much like the mysterious voice of the devil, so that all of a sudden the word 'devout' started to sound more like the word 'dissolute'. He was seized with panic at the thought that he had insulted the Mayor even though he had only spoken to himself. He could not be sure that the voice within him had been no more than a faint whisper. It could have been louder than he thought, and in that case one of the men standing around might have heard it saying that the Mayor was a dissolute man. He nodded his head and waved his hand as though chasing away the devil, muttering to himself, 'O Allah, I do take refuge in Thee against the accursed devil.'

'Yes, it's the devil,' said an angry voice nearby. 'Who would beat up our devout Sheikh Hamzawi other than the devil?'

'But he is no longer the Sheikh of our mosque,' commented a tall man who stood in the small crowd that was still hanging around.

'Allah has nothing to do with the likes of him,' added another voice in support of what the last man had said.

A short man with a meek face who had said nothing so far, took advantage of a sudden silence to ask in a low tone, 'But how can you say that, brother? What wrong has Sheikh Hamzawi done?'

'Don't you know what he did? Don't you live in this village? The worm has eaten our cotton, and we've had nothing but trouble since Sheikh Hamzawi gave shelter to that child of sin in his house. How can we allow a man who adopts the children of sin and fornication to lead us in prayer?'

The tall man was about to say, 'It's not the fault of the poor child,' but he swallowed quickly and kept silent at the sight of the anger glinting in many eyes. He remembered how his father used to repeat always that the children of sin only brought misfortune with them. He heard himself say in a voice which resembled that of his father, 'You're right, brother. The children of sin only bring misfortune with them,' then he swallowed again and rushed off to his field. A voice within him said, 'I'm a coward.' But he braced his shoulders and lifted his head and this time the voice sounded different when it said more loudly, 'He's right, children of sin only bring misfortune with them. Otherwise, why is it that we have had one problem after the other since Sheikh Hamzawi took that child into his house?'

As for Sheikh Hamzawi, he returned home to Fatheya, bleeding from his nose and mouth, his clothes dusty and torn, his head uncovered since he had lost his turban in the fight. Her mind told her that the life of her child was now in danger. She concealed him under her shawl and said, 'We can no longer live in this village.'

'I know no other place to live in,' responded Sheikh Hamzawi in a voice full of despair and exhaustion. 'I prefer to die here rather than in a strange place. There no one will lend us a helping hand.'

'Allah will take care of us, Hamzawi. Do you think He will abandon us to our fate?'

'I don't know,' said Sheikh Hamzawi. 'Allah seems to have abandoned me since I gave shelter to this child.'

'How can you repeat the same things that people in the village are saying?' protested Fatheya.

'Why does that surprise you? Aren't I like other people? Am I not human? I never pretended to be a saint, or a god.'

'What are you driving at, Hamzawi? If you don't want the child to stay, then before the sun rises tomorrow you will not find him here, and you will never see him again in this house. But I also will leave with him.'

'Do as you wish, Fatheya,' answered Sheikh Hamzawi in a weak voice. 'Go with him, or stay here, it no longer makes any difference. All I want out of life is that people should leave me alone.'

'I don't want to leave you alone,' she said, wiping the tears away with her hand, 'but people will give us no peace. Every time something goes wrong in the village, they will blame this poor, innocent child. What has the child got to do with the cotton worm, Hamzawi? Was it he who told the worm to eat the cotton? The brain of a buffalo has more sense in it than the mind of these people here in Kafr El Teen. But where can I go? I know no other village apart from Kafr El Teen.'

A few days passed and Fatheya forgot the questions she had asked herself. People no longer talked about them as they had done before. It looked as though they had forgotten the whole matter, or that what they had done to Sheikh Hamzawi was sufficient for them. And perhaps people would have forgotten. But one day the wind started to blow, and carried with it a spark from one of the ovens in which a woman was baking bread. The spark was very small, about the size of the head of a match, or maybe even smaller. It could have gone out had it landed on the dust-covered ground. But instead it flew on to one of the roofs, and landed while still partly alight on a heap of straw. If a gust of wind had happened to blow strongly at that moment, it might have put it out before it had time to ignite the straw. In fact, the wind went suddenly still, and during this time a small flame caught hold of one straw, so that when the wind started to blow again after a short while, the one straw was burning and the flames quickly caught hold of the whole heap, then moved quickly to the dung cakes and the cotton sticks jutting out as far as the roofs of the nearby houses.

It was not long before the villagers spotted the fire. The women slapped their faces and shrieked, the children screamed piercingly, adding to the clamour, and the men ran around in circles not knowing what to do. The village barber yelled out at them, 'Get pails of water, you animals!' but when the pails were brought the water never got anywhere near the flames. Each family started to count its children, lead the donkey or the buffalo out of the house, or extract the savings of a lifetime from some nook or hole in the wall.

The Chief of the Village Guard rushed off to the Mayor who had been informed of the fire by telephone. The red fire engine arrived after some time, its bell clanging. It was followed by the ambulance moving along behind. By then the children had tired of watching the fire, and turned to the fire engine with its ladder on which one could climb high up into the sky. As soon as it came to a stop they surrounded it on every side, standing on bare feet, their naked bottoms exposed from behind, their noses running in front. Swarms of flies kept settling on their faces or rising in black clouds.

Before the sun had dropped behind the line of treetops on the far side of the river everything in Kafr El Teen seemed to have returned to normal. Here and there wisps of smoke arose from a bare roof covered in black ashes. A child had suffocated in the smoke and lay dead on the mat close to the door where it had tried to crawl, and the frames of some windows were charred and black. On the dusty ground could be seen the imprint left behind by the wheels of the fire engine, but this was soon effaced by the cows, buffalo, donkeys and peasants returning in long lines from the fields after the day's work was over.

Fatheya remained wide awake with her arm tightly curled around the child. She could feel the danger which hovered around them, and kept her eyes close to the wall trying to catch what the villagers were saying. Deep down inside her she knew exactly what was going to happen now. And so when the words which were spoken reached her ears she felt no surprise at all. 'The fire would have consumed the whole village were it not for the grace of Allah. Since that son of fornication and sin descended on our village, we have had nothing but one misfortune after the other. It is time for us to do something about it.'

She felt her heart beating wildly, deep under the weak, distant pulse of the child she held to her chest, wrapped in her shawl. She opened the door slowly to make sure that none of the neighbours would hear it creak, then ran swiftly on bare feet until she had almost reached the river bank, but the eyes spotted her, and surrounded her on every side. She heard a wrathful voice call out, 'Where is the child, Fatheya?'

'He's not with me. He's asleep in the house,' she said, holding the little body tightly under her shawl.

'You are lying, Fatheya. The child is with you,' said the angry voice.

'No,' she said, 'it's not with me.' There was a shiver of terrible fear in the way she pronounced the denial.

She tried to slip away quickly, but a hand moved towards her and pulled the black shawl away, revealing the child as he lay close to her chest with his mouth holding to the nipple of her breast.

'It's my son. Don't take him away from me,' she shrieked with terror.

'He is born in fornication and we are a God-fearing people. We hate sin.'

A big rough hand stretched out in the dark to tear the child away from her, but it was as though she and the child had become one. Other hands moved towards her, trying to wrench the child away from her breast, but in vain. Her breast and the child had become inseparable.

The disc of the sun had by now disappeared completely and was no longer visible behind the line of trees on the opposite bank of the river. The night descended on the houses of Kafr El Teen like a heavy silent shadow, breathlessly still as though all life had suddenly ceased. The men high up on the bank moved hither and thither like dark spirits or ghosts which had emerged from the deep waters of the Nile. During the struggle for the child, Fatheya's clothes were torn away, and her body shone white, and naked, like that of a terrible mermaid in the moonlit night. Her face was as white as her body, and her eyes were filled with a strange, almost insane determination. She was soft, and rounded, and female and she was a wild animal, ferociously fighting those who surrounded her in the night. She hit out at the men with her legs, and her feet, with her shoulders and her hips all the while holding the child tightly in her arms.

Hands moved in on her from every side. They were big, rough hands with coarse fingers. The long black nails were like the black hoofs of buffalo and cows. They sank into her breast tearing flesh out of flesh. Male eyes gleamed with an unsatisfied lust, feeding on her breast with a hunger run wild like a group of starved men gathered around a lamb roasting on a fire. Each one trying to devour as much as he can lest his neighbour be quicker than him. Their hands moved like the quick paws of tigers or panthers in a fight, their eyes lit by an ancient vengeance, by some furious desire. In a few moments Fatheya's body had become a mass of torn flesh and the ground was stained red with her blood.

But after a while the river bank had become the same as it always was at night, no more than a part of the heavy, silent darkness that weighed down on everything, on the waters of the Nile, on the wide ribbon of land stretching along nearby, and on the dark mud huts and the winding lanes blocked with mounds of manure. The men of Kafr El Teen were now back in their houses, lying on the ground near their cattle and their wives like bodies without life or feeling. All except one man, Sheikh Hamzawi, who never closed his eyes that night, nor lay down to sleep. He kept his ear to the wall until all sound had ceased, and a deep silence had enveloped the village; a silence as dark and as terrifying as the silence of death. Then he stood up, walked towards the door of his house and opened it very carefully with a push of his shoulder so that it should not creak. He walked out into the lane, finding his way with the stick which he always used to ensure that his foot would not collide with a pebble, or a brick, or a dead cat which some boy had killed with a sling.

As he shuffled along slowly his stick hit something which his senses told him was not a stone, nor a brick, nor some small dead animal, but something still warm with the blood of life. He stopped short, and stood as still as a ghost, not moving one bit, so that even his yellow-beaded rosary ceased to go round between his fingers. His eyes were fastened on the naked body of his wife lying on the ground high up on the bank of the river.

Fatheya was moaning in a weak voice, and her breast still heaved up and down with a slow, irregular gasping movement.

He sat down beside her and took her hand between his own. 'Fatheya, Fatheya, it's Hamzawi,' he whispered.

She opened her bloodshot eyes and parted her lips slightly as though trying to say something, but no sound came out. He glimpsed someone approaching from a distance, took off his caftan, and covered her naked body with it. When the man came nearer, he recognized Sheikh Metwalli and said quickly, 'She is breathing her last. Can you carry her with me so that she can die in her bed?'

Sheikh Metwalli immediately bent over her ready to lift her bleeding body from the ground. But before they had time to take hold of her, she opened her eyes and looked around.

'She's looking for something,' said Sheikh Metwalli in a low voice.

'She's unconscious. Let's carry her to the house,' whispered back the old man, wiping the sweat from his brow.

But when they tried to lift her, the body of Fatheya held to the ground as though stuck with glue. Each time they tried to lift her, she would open her eyes and look around searching for something.

'She won't move. I'm sure she's looking for something,' said Sheikh Metwalli, his eyes probing here and there in the dark. Suddenly his eyes picked up a small shadow lying on the bank of the river, a short distance away. He went up to it, lifted it from the ground and came back carrying the torn body of her little child. Sheikh Metwalli held it out in his arms and laid it down softly on her chest. She curled her arms around it tightly and closed her eyes. And now when they lifted her they found that her body was light and easy to carry.

They carried her as far as the house, and on the following morning buried her with the child held tightly in her arms. Hamzawi bought her a shroud of green silk and they wrapped her in it carefully. They dug a long ditch for her and lay her softly down in it, then covered her with the earth which lay around. When it was over Metwalli wiped the sweat off his brow. His hand came away moist with something like tears when he touched his eyes. It was something which had never happened to him before, or at least he could not remember himself ever crying except perhaps when he was a child.

Only Allah and Sheikh Metwalli know that Fatheya's body and Fatheya's shroud both remained intact and unsoiled in the burial ground.

# XVI

He rested the big, hot palms of his two hands on the ground, and sat down with his back against the trunk of a tree, stretching out his legs as far as they could go. He had come a long distance, and they ached painfully. He could see his large feet against the setting sun. They were swollen, and the skin over them was cracked and inflamed.

He closed his eyes and tried to sleep, but they opened again. His look remained fastened on the endless ribbon of the river, with the fields rolling out beside it as far as his eyes could see. He was trying to find out where his world of Kafr El Teen began, to spot the first things he could recognize; the big mulberry tree where the river bank sloped down to the ditch, or to smell the odours he could pick out amongst a thousand other things: dust sprayed with water from the village stream, or wetted by the soft fruit of the mulberry tree, or dung mixed with the bran of bread from a hot oven, or his mother's shawl flapping in the wind when he walked beside her, or her breast when he slept on the mat huddled up against her in the winter nights.

For many years he had not smelt the odour of these things. He had left them behind in Kafr El Teen and gone away. He had never known these odours existed until the day he could smell them no more, until the day he donned his army uniform and became a private. He spent a long time not knowing that he had smelt them before, and they had a place in his life. During that time he slept in a small tent a few miles away from Suez, living with other odours, with the smell of bullets and shells fired from a gun, or burning leather, or conserves packed in rusty tins, or the sand of Sinai when planes unloaded their bombs on it, or winds unleashed their desert storms. But one night he opened his eyes just before dawn and suddenly there was that smell invading his nose. He did not recognize it on the spur of the moment, but it went through him with a strange happiness, like some drug which he might have swallowed or smoked. He was suddenly seized with a yearning to close his eyes and lay his head on his mother's breast. When he woke up in the morning he discovered that he had spent the night with a parcel she had sent him under his head. It was tied in a small bundle, and a colleague of his had carried it with him all the way from his village. Before opening the knot he brought it close to his nose, and for the first time recognized the odour with which he had lived for years in Kafr El Teen without ever having known it.

He breathed in the air blowing down between the river waters and the fields lying alongside, trying to detect the familiar odour of dust sprayed with muddy water from the nearby stream, but his nose failed to catch anything that smelt like it. He threw a searching glance in the same direction but nowhere could he find anything to indicate that he was near the approaches to Kafr El Teen.

He felt that the distance which lay before him might take long hours, or even days of walking. His lids closed over his eyes by a will stronger than his own. When they opened again, after a little while, he found the sun high up in the sky. A few moments went by before he realized that he had slept two days and two nights. He placed his palms flat on the ground and lifted his body upright. The skin of his palms was thick and coarse, and over it was the imprint of the groove made by his rifle. When he had paraded, or stood at attention or held the rifle to his shoulder and took aim it had rested in the groove made by long years of work with the hoe and dug it even deeper than before. When he stood up his body was like a bamboo cane, tall and thin, but his feet were swollen. Pus and blood oozed from the cracks in their skin, and the cracks had dark, muddy edges from miles and miles of walking. The burning disc of the sun was straight above his head and poured its rays down on him, and under the soles of his feet the ground was like hot needles. He could no longer tell where he was, for the Suez Canal was a strip of water and the hot needles under his feet was the silica sand of the retreat from Sinai cutting into his tortured skin.

His breath came in gasps, and before his eyes danced red circles. He closed his eyes to arrest the whirling movement. Suddenly there was an explosion. He knew the sound so well. It was terrifying like thunder, or an earthquake, or both, as though the sky and earth had collided. In less than a second he was lying curled up on the ground, with his chin tucked in, and his head held tightly protected under his arms. Then he crawled quickly over the ground looking for a ditch, or a hole, or a hollow between two sand dunes. There he lay on his belly perfectly still like a man who had died or was frozen.

The sound faded away and was replaced by a silence even deeper than before. He opened his eyes slowly, shooting frightened glances at the sky, looking for something flying high up. But there was nothing. No plane, or burning flame, no smoke, or cloudy greyness. Just the fiery disc of the sun burning down from above. His eyes dropped down from the sky and looked around, and when they ran over the river and the fields he realized he was no longer in the desert. The war was over, and he was returning home on foot to Kafr El Teen. The next moment he noticed that a group of children were gathered around him. They had seen him leap suddenly down the slope of the bank into the ditch. Behind swarms of flies their eyes were opened wide with surprise. He staggered away from them on his swollen feet. He could hear them laughing behind him. A shrill voice cried out, 'There goes the idiot.' Immediately the other children joined in and chanted in one voice, 'There goes the idiot.' Then they started to throw stones at him.

When he reached the outer limits of Kafr El Teen the sun had dropped behind the treetops on the other side of the river Nile. The dark night crept slowly over the low mud huts, and the lines of buffalo and cows slouched along the river bank on their way back home. Groups of peasants walked wearily behind, their backs bent by unceasing toil, their feet worn out from the daily coming and going.

Zakeya was already home. The buffalo was in the stable, while she squatted as usual near the door on the dusty threshold of her house with her back to the wall. She neither moved nor spoke. She did not even move her hand or nod her head. Her large black eyes stared into the night. It made no difference to her whether she kept awake or dozed, whether her eyes remained open or closed, for the night was always like a dark cloak. She did not know when she slept, or when she awoke, she did not know whether what she saw was real, or just another dream, or ghost. She could not tell whether the man who emerged in front of her at that moment was her brother Kafrawi or her son Galal. Her son Galal was not at all like her brother Kafrawi. The last image she had of him was the day they took him away to the army. She watched him walk away between two men. He was young then, and strong, and he walked upright with his eyes fixed on something he could see straight ahead. But the last image she had of Kafrawi was the day on which they had taken him away to gaol. He walked between two men, old-looking and bent, with his eyes on the ground. Yet now she did not know who of the two suddenly appeared before her eyes. The face was that of Galal, but the broken look in his eyes and the back which bent was without a doubt Kafrawi's.

She heard a voice like Galal's whisper in the dark. It sounded weak and spent. 'Mother... don't you recognize me? It's Galal. I'm back from Sinai.'

She continued to stare at him with her black eyes. She could not tell whether they were open or closed, whether this was real or a dream. She stretched out her hand to touch him. Whenever she used to grope for him in the night, his face would seem to fade away, and her fingers would clutch at a dark nothingness. But this time what she held was a hand of flesh and blood, a big warm hand just like Galal's. She brought it close to her face. It had the same smell as her breast, the same smell as her milk before it dried up. It was the smell of his hand, there was no doubt about that.

'My son, Galal, it's you!' she whispered in a weak, husky voice burying her face in his hand.

'Yes, mother, it's Galal,' he said, bowing his head. She touched his head and neck, his shoulders and his arms, his legs and his feet with her big rough hands. She was making sure that there was no wound, no part missing, making sure he was whole.

'Are you all right, my son?' she whispered.

'Yes, mother,' he said. 'I'm all right. And you? Are you well, mother?'

'Yes, my son. I'm well.'

'But you're not the same as you were when I left you,' he said, looking at her with anxious eyes.

'That's four years ago. It's time, son,' she said. 'Time, and you too, Galal, you are not the same.'

'It's nothing,' he said. 'I'm tired from the long distance I walked. It was very long. I need to rest.'

He lay down next to her on the dust-covered ground. She rubbed his feet in warm water and salt, then wrapped them in her shawl. His eyes were wide open, staring at the ceiling of the mud hut. She squatted next to him, and her lips were tightly closed. At one moment she parted them slightly as though about to tell him the story of what had happened, but she closed them again and kept silent. But after a while she heard him ask, 'How is my uncle, Kafrawi?'

She was silent for a long moment before she said, 'He is well.'

'And Nefissa? And Zeinab?'

She hesitated for a moment, then in an almost inaudible voice said, 'They are well. Do you wish to eat something? You probably haven't put anything in your mouth for days.'

She got up and went to fetch the basket of bread, a piece of old cheese, and salted pickles. Then walking towards the door she said, 'I will go to buy you a piece of sesame sweet from the shop of Haj Ismail.'

He realized she was hiding something from him and looked at her with an increased anxiety. 'I do not want to eat. Come, sit here and tell me what's been happening. You're hiding something. You're not the same as when I left you.'

Her eyes avoided his, staring at something in the dark. She was silent for some time, then he heard her whisper, 'Nefissa has run away.'

There was another long silence as heavy and as oppressive as the surrounding darkness lying over the village. Once again her lips parted to let out the same whisper. 'And Kafrawi is in gaol.'

This time she closed her lips as though she intended never to open them again. After a long moment she heard him ask in a low voice which rose from somewhere hidden deep in the dark, 'And Zeinab?'

His voice wavered when he pronounced her name, wavered with a hesitation, with wanting to ask and fearing the answer, with wanting to know and afraid of what would be revealed. A strange feeling had come over him the moment he saw her face, a feeling that something terrible had happened while he was far away. Kafrawi was his uncle, and Nefissa his cousin. But Zeinab had always meant something different to him. Every time he heard her voice calling out to her Aunt Zakeya something within him quivered. When their eyes met he would feel his legs go weak under him, as though his muscles had tired suddenly and needed rest. He longed to lay his head on her breast and close his eyes. If he got a glimpse of her bare legs as she sat with his mother in front of the oven, he would be seized with a strong desire to carry her away from under the watchful eyes to where he could close a door on her and hold her in his arms.

His mother could feel what was going on in him, sense his voice tremble when he called out to Zeinab, notice how his eyes searched for the girl when she was out in the fields. She could feel him burn with an obscure desire when he heard her voice before she came into the house, and watched the warm blood slowly suffuse his dark face when the girl squatted down beside her.

One night when he lay close to her on the mat she heard a stifled groan. She whispered in the dark, 'What's wrong with you, Galal?'

'I want Zeinab my cousin,' he replied without opening his eyes.

'We will marry her to you, my son, when you come back from the army,' she said, patting him on the head like a child.

But now Zakeya stayed silent. He raised his bowed head and looked at her in the dark, and although he could not see her face, he sensed her eyes staring at the iron gate which rose up in the night some distance away from their house.

He asked her again, this time trying hard to conceal the trembling in his voice. 'And Zeinab? What did she do once her father and her sister were no longer in the house?'

'She started to work in the Mayor's house.'

He could not prevent his voice from trembling as he asked, 'What does she do?'

'She washes, and sweeps and cleans the house.'

His whole body started to shiver as he asked again, 'And where does she spend the night?'

'She spends it here with me, my son. She's asleep now, on top of the oven.'

He swallowed quickly. The shiver in his body gradually subsided. He rested his hands on the floor, then paused for a moment before getting up. 'Have you got a clean *galabeya* for me, mother?'

'Yes my son. We've kept the new *galabeya* you had made before leaving for the army.'

He felt as though he was coming back to life. 'Heat me some water. I want to take a bath,' he said.

# XVII

As soon as the Chief of the Village Guard entered the room where the Mayor was sitting he realized at once why he had sent for him. Since the day when Galal had married Zeinab, Sheikh Zahran had been expecting this moment to come. He had voiced his fears to Haj Ismail but the village barber tried to set his mind at rest. 'Don't worry, Sheikh Zahran. Galal has come back from the war a broken man, and he won't dare defy the Mayor. As a matter of fact, he should feel proud that his wife is working for the most important man in our village.'

'You don't know Galal as well as I know him,' said Sheikh Zahran. 'He's one of those stupid men who wax jealous over their wives. And ever since the girl was a child, he's been in love with her.'

'Since he's stupid, he won't be assailed by doubts about anything. It's only intelligent people who wonder about things,' commented Haj Ismail.

'But he's refused to send his wife to the Mayor's house,' said Sheikh Zahran.

'Stupid people like him prefer to eat dry bread and salt, rather than send their wives to work as servants in a house. They think a servant's work is shameful.'

'But this is not just any house! It's the Mayor's house,' objected Sheikh Zahran.

'Stupid people don't differentiate between houses, Sheikh Zahran. To them a house is a house.'

'What do we do if he stops Zeinab from going?'

'Don't start worrying right from now,' said the village barber. 'Maybe the Mayor will have had enough of her by then, and won't want her to go to him any more. You know he gets bored very quickly, and none of these girls has lasted with him very long.'

But the fears of Sheikh Zahran proved to be justified, and the day came when the Mayor said to him, in a voice which brooked no discussion, 'Go, and come back with Zeinab.'

So Sheikh Zahran and Haj Ismail sat in front of the shop smoking the water-jar pipe while they pondered over the problem.

'You don't know Galal like I do,' kept repeating Sheikh Zahran. 'It's true he's an idiot just like the rest of these village men in Kafr El Teen. But we can't be sure that he hasn't learnt a few things since he joined the army, and went to Misr. Don't forget he's lived with soldiers all these years. I doubt if he can be fooled with amulets any more. We have to think of something else from now on.'

'Men in this village are cowards, but they have no shame. Put fear in his heart, Sheikh Zahran. You know how to do that.'

'That's true. But with men like Galal, I prefer to do things without using force. You don't know him well enough. He's not like Kafrawi, and for all you know, he could start creating a lot of problems in the village. Things are getting worse, and people have started to open their eyes much more than before. Prices are rising all the time and the peasants owe more and more taxes to the government. The Mayor is no longer as popular as he was at one time.'

'But you've tried convincing him before and failed,' said Haj Ismail. 'Now you have no choice but to use a bit of force.'

Sheikh Zahran was silent for a long time as though lost in thought. Haj Ismail waited patiently for a while, but then, unable to contain himself any more, he asked, 'What are you thinking of, Sheikh Zahran?'

'I'm thinking of the easiest way. I don't want to use force,' answered Sheikh Zahran.

Haj Ismail looked at him for a long moment before he said in a quiet voice, 'Are you afraid of Galal, Sheikh Zahran?'

The Chief of the Village Guard twirled his whiskers. 'Galal does not frighten me. But somehow this time I feel that something's going to happen. I don't know exactly what, but my mind is not at rest. People have changed, Haj Ismail. The people who at one time could not look me in the eye, now look at me straight in the face, and no longer bow their heads to the ground when I pass by. Just yesterday, one of the villagers refused to pay his taxes and shouted, "We work all the year round and all we end up with are debts to the government." I never used to hear this kind of talk from any of them before. The peasants are getting more and more hungry. All they have to eat is some dry bread and wormy salted cheese. And hunger makes a man blind. It makes him see no one, neither ruler nor God. Hunger breeds heretics, Haj Ismail.'

'They've always been hungry. There's nothing new in that, and the villagers have always lived on dry bread and salted cheese with worms. They've never known anything else.' He fell silent for a moment, and then resumed as though an idea had occurred to him. 'Sheikh Zahran, instead of trying to frighten him, have you thought of trying to tempt him with something really worthwhile? Zakeya and Galal are up to their ears in debt and you are the one who is supposed to collect the taxes they owe to the government. If you suggest to Galal that you might be prepared to be lenient, it could go a long way to making him less obstinate.'

'You have no idea all the things I've attempted with Galal since I found out he'd married Zeinab,' said Sheikh Zahran. 'If I could have stopped the marriage, I would have, but I learnt about it after everything was over. Since then I knew the day would come when the Mayor would send for me to bring Zeinab back, I tried to convince Galal that there was no need for him to stop her from going to the Mayor's house, but he told me that it was she who had refused to go back.'

'Who of the two do you think is refusing?' asked Haj Ismail.

'Most probably it's his influence, since she continued to work for the Mayor until she got married,' answered Sheikh Zahran.

'She must really love him. Or perhaps she feels it's a sin to go to the Mayor's house now that she's married.'

'In any case,' said Sheikh Zahran, 'it's clear that the presence of Galal at her side is an encouragement for her to refuse.'

'Then what did you do after that?'

'After that,' said Sheikh Zahran, 'I tried what you suggested before. I told him we could reduce the taxes he has to pay to the government, but he didn't seem to be interested at all. Now I have no other alternative but to use my authority.'

'But what can you do?'

'He will either pay his debts immediately or else we will confiscate his land.'

'But the land is life to a peasant,' said Haj Ismail. 'If you confiscate it, it's like taking their life. Besides, you might find yourself in a corner if you apply this only to Galal. All the peasants owe taxes to the government so why only him? You had better think of something else, Sheikh Zahran.'

Sheikh Zahran did not proffer any answer. The only way out he could now see was to get rid of Galal in one way or another. He had got rid of Kafrawi by arranging things in such a way that he was accused of a crime and ended in gaol. He continued to scratch his wits in order to find a solution.

Haj Ismail could not hear the questions that were being asked in Sheikh Zahran's mind, but one look at his face was enough to tell him the direction in which his thoughts were moving. They both lapsed into a long silence. All that could be heard was the gurgling sound of the water-jar pipe, or the noise which Haj Ismail made when he cleared his nose and his throat every now and then. The dark night had by now enveloped Kafr El Teen in its heavy cloak, and the air hardly moved over the surface of the river. The sombre mud huts and the winding lanes seemed to sink into a silence as still and profound as the silence of death, as the end of all movement.

# XVIII

Zakeya was sitting as still as usual on the dusty threshold of her house, her black eyes watching the lane, and the iron gate with its iron bars, when she heard the noise of many voices, and saw a group of men enter through the doorway, preceded by the Chief of the Village Guard. His voice rang out in the small yard, 'Search the house!'

Before she had time to ask what they wanted, or to understand what was going on, the men had started to move around the small mud hut searching everywhere, behind the doors, on top of the oven, and up on the roof, and in every gap or hole, no matter how small. She stood watching them with an almost dazed look in her wide open eyes. After a while a man appeared carrying a small bundle. He walked up to the Chief of the Village Guard and said, 'We've found it, Sheikh Zahran. He had hidden it on top of the oven.'

The Chief of the Village Guard shouted at the top of his voice, 'The thief! Arrest him immediately. Where is your son, Zakeya?'

'He's in the fields,' she said in a frightened voice. 'What do you want of him? What has he done?'

'Your son Galal is a big thief, Zakeya. He stole this from the Mayor's house,' said Sheikh Zahran, holding out the small bundle. 'Look!' he added, opening it. 'It's full of silver coins.'

She was seized with a feeling of bewilderment soon overcome by her increasing terror at the sight of hundreds of silver coins flashing in the light of the kerosene lamps. But she cried out defiantly, 'My son does not steal, Sheikh Zahran, and he's never been to the Mayor's house.'

Sheikh Zahran's lips twisted into a sneer, which he followed with an ironic, snorting laugh. 'You know nothing about your son, or else you're just pretending that you don't know what he has done. Are you sure he said nothing to you about this bundle?'

'No, Sheikh Zahran,' she answered quickly. 'I know nothing. And my son Galal is certainly not the one who stole these coins.'

The Chief of the Village Guard gave another prolonged snort and asked, 'Then, pray tell me, who stole them, Zakeya, and who hid them on top of your oven. A spirit?'

She slapped her face several times with both her hands and cried out, 'Never, never. My son Galal is not a thief. You will not take him away from us as you did with Kafrawi.'

But they took him. Galal could not understand what was happening. He was taken straight from the field to the police station, in the same *galabeya* he was wearing as he worked. From that moment onwards they kept moving him from one room to another and asking him questions all the time. He walked as though in a dream and from the look in his eyes it was clear that he could not make out a thing of what was going on around him. He felt he was living in a nightmare. He did not know what to answer when they questioned him and all he would say was, 'I don't know anything. I don't know why I'm here. I don't know anything about this bundle. I've never been to the Mayor's house.'

But then they brought the witnesses. One of them was the Chief of the Village Guard in person. There was a witness to say that he had seen him running out of a back door in the Mayor's house. There was a second witness who was sure he had been carrying something which looked like a small bundle. Still a third one maintained that he had called out to him at the time when he had been seen, but instead of answering, he had continued to run until he disappeared through a door opposite the Mayor's house. The Chief of the Village Guard was the last of the witnesses to speak. He said that he had always held Galal in high esteem as a soldier who had done his duty defending the land of his forefathers, and always felt that he could trust him and have confidence in him. But faced with the things which had been brought to his notice, he had been obliged to search the house in which Galal lived. Then after a short pause he added that this was the first time Galal had stolen. He could not understand what had driven him to do so except perhaps that he owed the government a lot of arrears in taxes, and was obliged to pay at least a part of the debt, otherwise the government authorities would have taken the measures that are normal in such cases.

It was clear that the Chief of the Village Guard knew exactly what to say when dealing with the police. He was well versed in their language and they too understood what he was trying to say.

As soon as he was finished the magistrate turned to Galal and asked, 'Have you got anything to say for yourself?'

'I know nothing about this bundle,' he repeated for the hundredth time. The sweat poured from his brow and he looked around him in a daze. 'I never entered the Mayor's house,' he added.

But they sent him off to gaol. He found himself in a narrow room crowded with other people, and he could hardly breathe, or move. When his eyes got accustomed to the absence of light he began to look around. He could see the sallow faces tanned to the hue of dark leather. The eyes were black and large, and they looked at him with the expression of men who have resigned themselves to their fate, and given up fighting a long time ago. For a moment he felt he had seen the face of his uncle Kafrawi. He whispered, 'Uncle Kafrawi?'

But a voice answered in the dark, 'Who's Kafrawi, my son?'

# XIX

When they came to take Galal away, Zeinab held on to his arm and shrieked, 'Don't take my husband away from me. Take me with him.' But the rough strong hands of the men pushed her aside and Galal was driven away in the small van.

She said not one word for three days, nor did she go to the fields, nor lead the buffalo by the rope tied around its neck, as it plodded behind her. She did not even go to the river to fill the earthenware jar with water, or cook, or bake bread. She just sat beside her Aunt Zakeya on the dusty threshold of her house, her eyes silently following the way the van had taken when it carried Galal off to gaol.

On the third day she stood up, went to the stable, took out the buffalo, and left the house leading it behind her. She returned without the buffalo, but between her breasts she was hiding a small handkerchief knotted around a few coins. When she arrived she squatted down beside her Aunt Zakeya without saying anything.

On the fourth day at the crack of dawn she stood up again and went out alone. She continued to walk until she reached the place where the bus stopped. She took it to Bab El Hadeed and then asked a passer-by where she could find the gaol. Along the way she kept asking different people until she reached a station. There she took a train and when she got down walked again until she found herself standing in front of the huge prison door. But the man at the gate told her that visits were forbidden without written permission.

She asked, 'How do I get a permit to visit my husband in the gaol?'

The man explained, and after he had explained she walked back along the same way, took a train and managed to get back to Bab El Hadeed. There she found a tram which dropped her in front of a huge building full of people, and desks, and papers. She entered the building and was swallowed up with the other people. Inside she went from room to room until it was time to leave. And this went on for several days. She felt she was going round and round in an endless journey. After some time the money she had with her was finished. A kind man met her on the way out. He was one of those men who helped women in need to spend the night in the mosque of Al Sayeda. But instead of taking her to the mosque he took her to spend the night with him in his room.

After that no one in Kafr El Teen heard anything more about Zeinab.

# XX

Since the day they had taken Galal away and Zeinab had gone after him, Zakeya continued to sit on the dusty ground of the entrance to her house without moving or saying a thing. Her eyes stared into the night with a terrible anger like the anger of some wild beast being hunted down. In her mind something was happening very slowly, something like thinking, like a tiny point of light appearing in a dark sky. At moments it would be there and at others it disappeared. She groped in her mind for this tiny star in the infinite night like someone searching for the tip of the thread in a tangled reel of cotton, but it always managed to escape her.

But the darkness of her mind was no longer the same. It had changed. Nor was her mind the same mind it had been before. Something had started to move in it, a tiny flitting thing. And a question kept whispering under the bones in her skull, a question she had never asked before, and which grew louder all the time until it became like a ringing bell. If it was not Galal, and of that she was sure, who was it then?

She suddenly remembered the day when the Mayor sent for Zeinab. Since the girl had married she had vowed to Allah never to set foot in the Mayor's house. Kneeling on the prayer carpet she said to Him, 'I did what Thou willed me to do, O God, and I thank Thee for curing my Aunt Zakeya. Now I am a wife lawfully married according to the *Sunna* of Allah and His prophet, and I will never go there again.' And that night she heard a voice from heaven say to her, 'Yes Zeinab, you are a wife now, and Allah forbids you to go there again.'

It was as though this new awareness had given her a strength which nothing could overcome. No power on earth could any longer convince her to go to the Mayor's house. When the Chief of the Village Guard came to her, she insisted, 'No, I will not go. I refuse to disobey Allah, Sheikh Zahran.'

'But who told you that if you go back to the Mayor's house you will be disobeying Allah? On the contrary, it was Allah who ordered you to go to the Mayor's house, was it not?' asked Sheikh Zahran.

'That was before I married,' cried out Zeinab. 'Now I am a wife and Allah has forbidden me to go there.'

Zakeya was sitting in her usual place listening to what was being said. Suddenly another tiny star lit up in the darkness of her head. She could not grasp anything at the beginning but a slow movement kept going through her mind, and once it started it went on slowly at first, then a little faster. For once she had started to think, it had to go on. She had caught the top of the thread between her fingers and now the reel would keep turning and turning until it reached the end, no matter how long.

Soon another question started to flit through her mind in a subdued whisper which became louder and louder. So in the middle of one night, the night after Galal had gone to gaol,

Zeinab felt her Aunt Zakeya give her a violent nudge with her fist, as she lay on the mat beside her. When she looked into the old woman's eyes a shiver went through her spine. They were wide open and something terrible seemed to be going on inside them. She heard her whisper in a strange, hoarse voice, 'Zeinab! Zeinab!'

She whispered back, 'What's wrong, Aunt?'

'I was blind, but now my eyes have been opened.'

'You were never blind,' said Zeinab, shivering all over at the look in her aunt's eyes. 'Your eyes were perfect. But tell me what's wrong?'

For a moment she thought that her aunt had fallen sick again. She clasped her hand and said, 'Lie down, please lie down, Aunt. You are tired. Since they took Galal away you have not slept.'

But the fearsome look in her eyes was still there, almost like a madness, and her voice continued its hoarse whisper.

'I know who it is. I know, Zeinab. I know.'

'Who is it?' asked Zeinab at a loss, and still shivering all over.

'It's Allah, Zeinab, it's Allah,' she said in a distant tone as though her mind had strayed far away.

Zeinab was now shaking violently all over. She took hold of her aunt's hand. It was as cold as ice.

'Ask Allah to have mercy on you. Do your ablutions and pray, so that Allah may forgive us both, and have pity on us.'

'Do not say that, Zeinab. You know nothing,' she cried out in sudden anger. 'I am the one who knows.'

# XXI

Zakeya continued to squat at the entrance to her house with her eyes wide open, staring steadily into the night. Now she never slept, or even closed her eyes. They pierced the darkness to the other side of the lane where rose the huge iron gate of the Mayor's house. She did not know exactly what she was waiting for. But as soon as she saw the blue eyes appear between the iron bars she stood up. She did not know why she stood up instead of continuing to squat, nor what she would do after that. But she walked to the stable and pushed the door open. In one of the corners she noticed the hoe. Her tall, thin body approached and bent over it. Her hand was rough and big, with a coarse skin, and it held the hoe in a firm grip as her big, flat feet walked out of the door. She paused for a moment then crossed the lane to the iron gate. The Mayor saw her come towards him. 'One of the peasant women who work on my farm,' he thought. When he came close he saw her arm rise high up in the air holding the hoe.

He did not feel the hoe land on his head and crush it at one blow. For a moment before, he had looked into her eyes, just once. And from that moment he was destined never to see, or feel, or know anything more.

# XXII

The grey van advanced over the road with Zakeya squatting inside just as she used to squat at the entrance to her house. It sped along streets and roads she had never seen before, or even realized could exist. It was a different world to the world she had known. From a crack in the wood covering the window she could see a river, like the Nile in Kafr El Teen, but to her it did not look like the Nile. The van stopped in front of a huge door. She walked surrounded by the men who had brought her. Around her wrists they had put handcuffs but her large black eyes were wide open. Her lips were tightly closed as though she did not want to say anything, or could not remember words any longer. But every now and then the men around her could see her mutter, like someone talking to herself. She kept repeating in a low voice, 'I know who it is. Now I know him.' In the middle of the night, as she lay on the floor of her cell near the other women prisoners, her lids would remain wide open. She stared into the dark with open eyes but her lips were always tightly closed. But one of the prisoners heard her mutter in a low voice, 'I know who it is.' And the woman asked her curiously, 'Who is it, my dear?'

And Zakeya answered, 'I know it's Allah, my child.'

'Where is He?' sighed her companion. 'If He were here, we could pray Him to have mercy on women like us.'

'He's over there, my child. I buried him there on the bank of the Nile.'